LIMIT YOUR GREED

Put principles above money to build
better businesses and a better world
(and still make a profit)

by

Mark L. Van Name and

Bill Catchings

LYG, LLC
10024 Sycamore Road
Raleigh, NC 27613
www.lyg.org

ISBN: 978-0-9995829-0-9

First printing, December 2017

Printed in the United States of America

*For everyone who works at
Principled Technologies.*

*We're proud to be
your colleagues.*

CONTENTS

PART THREE: Challenges and opportunities

PART FOUR: Afterwords

INTRODUCTION

make the world a better place

We want you to help us make the world a better place. We want to do it by building better businesses.

This book is for business owners—but it's not just for them. You don't need to be starting a business or the owner of an existing company to benefit from it. You can bring the book's ideas to where you work, and to friends, and even to strangers. Your employer could benefit from them. The businesses of others could do the same. *Everyone* can help build better businesses by starting conversations and showing how it's possible both to take better care of all employees and to make a healthy profit.

At the heart of this book are two simple but powerful ideas.

The first is the notion of limiting your greed, *choosing*—we don't want anyone to force anyone else to do anything—to take less so that others can have more. This idea is particularly relevant to those who own and run businesses, but it's also important to people at all levels in all organizations. We're not talking here about working for free or building non-profits; we want people to earn good incomes, and we want businesses to make money. What we're suggesting is that by putting limits on your compensation so that everyone else in a business can reap more of its rewards, and by treating yourself just as you treat all other employees, you can help a lot of people, make the world better, and in many ways get back more than you give.

Limiting your greed is hard, particularly at first, because you're absolutely choosing to take less money than you might otherwise have gotten. Our experience has shown, though, that by doing so, you create a more successful company, one with happier and more motivated employees, and one more likely to succeed—and thus to continue to reward you.

The second concept is equally simple and powerful: businesses don't have to do things the ways they've always been done. New solutions to old problems are frequently possible, and those solutions can help a business be both successful and rewarding to all its employees. The key is to be willing to think differently rather than simply conform to existing common practices.

In this book, we show many ways to put these concepts into action in the real world. These are not theories, not ideas we hatched while thinking about business in the abstract. We have lived them since January 2003, when we started a company, Principled Technologies, that we hoped would be unlike traditional businesses.

That business is still running and growing and successful today. The ideas in this book are not wild-eyed notions; they *work*.

Of course, if everything about the way businesses

operate and treat their employees today seems right to you, then this book may not be for you.

If, though, like so many of us you wonder if things couldn't be different, couldn't be better, then read on. We'll show you how a lot of questions led to a lot of answers that are working in the real world, and we'll provide tools you can use to formulate your own questions and answers. We don't have all the answers, and different businesses may require different solutions, but we can share what we've learned over the last fifteen years.

In the first part of the book, we'll use the principles upon which we based our business to show some of the many ways you can help build better businesses.

In the second, we'll examine how we created that company by rethinking pretty much everything, and we'll share the specific solutions we chose. Whether those notions work for you or don't fit well, they at least point out some of the possible improvements.

In the third and final part, we'll examine the challenges and opportunities you're likely to face as your business grows, some of the issues we've faced, and some possible solutions. These challenges never stop, because each time a business grows and evolves, it faces new ones.

we can build better businesses and a better world

Above all else, our experiences have taught us one

lesson: we can indeed do better. If we all work at it, together we can build better businesses and a better world—and still make a profit and a very good living in the process.

PART ONE

Principles

LIMIT YOUR GREED

CHAPTER 1

passionate about and proud of

A few years after we started PT, a successful young friend working in the finance industry asked one of us about starting his own business. We told him not to do so just because he might be able to make more money; that's not enough of a foundation for a great company. Instead, we advised him to start something new only if he felt passionate about doing so, compelled to do it. He was accustomed to the support structures of a big company. With a new company, we warned him, everything falls on the founders' shoulders, so your passion needs to be part of what will sustain you.

When we were starting PT, we believed that any business we built had to be something we were both passionate about and proud of. We had both worked plenty of jobs that lacked one or both of those characteristics.

Though we had left our previous employer, needed a way to make money, and hoped to earn good incomes, we wanted to do more than that. We wanted not only to start a new company, but also to create something that reflected our principles, priorities, and personalities. We strongly believed, and still believe, that pride and passion are the best motivators. Fear, guilt, ambition, and a host of other factors can motivate people, but passion and pride will carry you farther than most.

What, we asked ourselves, could we be passionate about?

We'd had our fill of traditional businesses. We found that we were passionate about the notion of creating a company that would not only be profitable but would also serve as a social experiment, one that approached business differently. We wanted to build a place that had strong underlying principles in its DNA. We wanted a company that was willing to question everything about the way other organizations did business.

> **Fear, guilt, ambition, and a host of other factors can motivate people, but passion and pride will carry you farther than most.**

On a more practical level, we were both passionate about technology. We both loved playing with the latest computers and gadgets. We had spent over fifteen years working in the technology trade press evaluating computers and related technologies. For us, technology was, and still is, the obvious choice for where to work.

We knew what we could be passionate about, but what could we be proud of?

We felt we would be proud of a business that took satisfaction in doing great work for its clients. While profits are essential to a successful business, we wanted to focus on doing work that led to happy customers. Old-fashioned customer service mattered to us. We wanted our focus to be first and foremost on our clients.

We also felt we could be proud of a business that took care of its people, that made them a top priority. We had plenty of experiences with companies that gave lip service to that goal but did little to reach it. One example that has always stayed with us was a meeting in which several department heads had to give their biggest triumph and disappointment of the previous month. One of them counted laying off half a receptionist as the month's triumph. Putting aside how it's even possible to lay off half a person, it was galling that a layoff was a triumph rather than a disappointment. We knew our company must never see a layoff, even an unavoidable one, as anything other than a failure.

The combination of principles we could be proud of and technology we were passionate about led quite naturally to the company's name, Principled Technologies.

Our next challenge was to figure out how to build this business. The obvious place to start was where most businesses begin: a clear mission statement.

Or, maybe not.

LIMIT YOUR GREED

CHAPTER 2

a clear existence statement

Business leaders like to create mission statements, short declarations that explain the organization's primary goals. If you're going to build a business based on a different set of guiding principles, however, start with an even more basic statement: an existence statement, the reason the business exists at all. Why are you starting a business? Or, for established businesses, why did this company come into being and, perhaps more importantly, why does it still exist today?

Yes, you can start a company simply as a way to make money, but if you want to build something different, something better, that reason alone won't cut it.

If you're in an existing business, you're dealing with a sort of corporate organism that wants by its very existence to keep on being; businesses, like most social structures, want to stay alive. Many businesses go against this corporate instinct by selling themselves to other businesses and thus losing their identity, but the instinct to survive is strong in most organizations.

Simple survival, though, should not be the reason a business exists.

If you're clear and honest about your company's reasons for existence, and if you always keep them in mind, those reasons can serve as foundational principles for the business and as key factors in decisions that shape your path into the future.

When we started PT, we knew we were going to build a service business related to technology, and we knew a fair amount about the services we were going to provide. We didn't want to create a fancy mission statement, but we did want to remind ourselves constantly why we were starting this particular company. After a lot of thought and discussion, the reason for PT's existence boiled down to one sentence with two parts:

Do great work for our clients, and be a great place to work for our staff.

> Do great work for our clients, and be a great place to work for our staff.

These two phrases are broad enough that it's tempting to dismiss them as useless platitudes. What company, after all, doesn't want to do great work or to be great for its employees? Everyone, it might seem, would agree with these goals.

They might agree, but most would not build businesses around them.

As reasons to exist, these two phrases become more than just goals or principles. They provide focus. They define priorities. And what they don't mention proves to be almost as vital as what they do.

They tell us that above all else, we are to focus first on our clients. Customers are not a necessary evil; they are why the business exists. Doing great work for our clients means putting ourselves in their shoes, listening carefully to them and valuing what they say, doing our very best to understand their needs, and figuring out the best ways to meet those needs.

Our business would exist to serve its customers. It would constantly concentrate on delivering ever better services to them and on making it easier for them to work with us. Our goal would never be to extract the maximum possible money from them; their needs would come first. Yes, we would expect to receive payment for the work we did for them, but by placing them first, we would always strive to make that cost reasonable and fair for them and for us.

As the first phrase of our existence statement makes clear, it is not enough to serve our clients; we have to provide great service for them. Implicit in that statement is the need to hire a great team to do the complex work behind the services, to produce services that meet their specific requirements, and so on. A lot follows directly from those few words.

Because we work in technology, the most rapidly evolving sector of the economy, the statement also implies the need for constant change, for adaptation to a rapidly mutating universe of products and needs. If our company couldn't change quickly and adapt to deal with an ever-shifting market, it wouldn't be able to do great work for its clients.

The second phrase of the existence statement puts the rest of our focus on our staff. The business exists to serve them, too. Giving them jobs is not enough. We have to think about all the ways in which we can make the company a great place for them to work. We must consider the effect on them of every single decision we are contemplating. We have to listen to them as carefully as we listen to our clients, learn their needs, and try to meet them. Caring about our colleagues is not just a part of a mission; it is a core reason the business exists.

Priorities are easy to see when the founding principles are this simple and clear. The clients come first. We who work at the company are a very close second. Most of the time, there's no conflict between the two priorities. When, however, we as a company have to choose between doing something great for our clients or taking the easier path for ourselves, the choice is obvious: we do what's great for our clients.

This existence statement also made clear the roles of the leaders, initially us: we were by virtue of starting the company its heads, but we were also and more importantly servants and students. Our job was to serve our clients and our fellow employees. We might be the leaders of this new tribe, but because the company existed to serve its clients and its staff, our jobs should be primarily about taking care of all the members of that tribe. Further, as students, we had to put aside our preconceptions as much as possible and instead listen and learn what each group wanted and needed.

As we noted above, the many things this existence statement does *not* mention are also vital. Nowhere does it talk about the owners making the most possible money, or maximizing return for shareholders, or trying to make the largest possible profit. Most businesses today have maximizing shareholder value as their top priority. Doing what will make the owners—the shareholders—the most money is often in conflict with doing the very best work for the company's customers. At PT, nothing about maximizing value for shareholders is why the business exists, so we avoid that conflict.

The existence statement also does not contain an exit strategy, the way that we as founders would one day reap value from the business. Some people, for example, start businesses with the intent of taking them public, or with the hope of one day being acquired. We very consciously chose to start PT without any such strategy. Making the business do great work for its clients and be a great place to work for its people was enough of a challenge; the rest, we trusted, would come in time. If the primary reason for a business' existence is to achieve some exit strategy for the shareholders so they can make a lot of money, that business has already lost a bit of its direction—maybe even a bit of its soul—before it starts.

None of this is to say, of course, that the business should not make money. It must. Without income, any business ends quickly. Without a profit, in the short term the business will have to turn to investors or loans to secure the cash it needs to operate, and in the long term, it will fail. No matter how much we might want to rethink the ways our business would operate, we don't get to ignore these basics, at least not in the long term.

We've learned that it's vital to use the existence statement to make sure you always focus on the most important goals. For us at PT, as simple as our existence statement is, we keep returning to it for guidance. Its focus, its inherent priorities, and the implications of all the things it doesn't mention continue to guide us to this day.

Another key component on which most companies, particularly those in tech, depend is the business plan, a set of goals for growth and a plan for taking the business forward. After all, every new company needs a business plan, right?

CHAPTER 3

no targets for growth

We had prepared plenty of business plans in the past, so creating one for PT seemed like an obvious step. When you're committed to rethinking everything about a business, however, you must resist doing anything by reflex. Instead, you should question why that thing is worth doing.

So, we asked ourselves, why do you create business plans?

A common reason is to state clear goals for the business, to set the measures by which you could later tell if it was succeeding. If you exist to serve your clients and your employees, however, your primary measures should be how happy your clients and staff are, whether you truly are doing great work for your clients and being a great place to work for your staff. Financial and size goals would be more distractions than aids.

One could argue that profit and revenue growth are great ways to measure client happiness, but those two indicators can be quite misleading. A new product or offering might earn a lot for you for a while but leave a wake of dissatisfied customers who won't be coming back. In addition, maximizing profit was not a goal, so measuring success that way made no sense.

Another reason to create a business plan is to understand your capital requirements. You're going to need money to run a business, and that means you're going to need investors. Investors will quite reasonably want a good return on their investment, and so they will typically demand a plan that shows them how the company will deliver that return. Even if you manage somehow to find investors who don't want to maximize the return on their investment, they will need *some* return. After all, that is why they invest!

We had no desire for investors. Worse, serving their needs would have been a distraction, an expenditure of time and energy that would not help the business live up to its existence statement.

We also knew that if we let in other owners, which investors would be, we would immediately open ourselves to an understandable pressure to do things the way businesses normally do them. We didn't want that.

We were lucky enough to be able to start a company without external capital. Not everyone will be that fortunate. Sometimes, you can build to that situation by investing a lot of your time and energy, an approach often known as putting in "sweat equity." If, though, you must take outside funds to start a business, then you either have to find the most compatible possible investors or borrow the funds. In those cases, you are very likely to have to develop a business plan.

For us, each time we considered a reason for creating a business plan, we came to the same conclusion: such a plan would contribute no value to us and would instead both waste energy and take our attention off more important matters. We wanted to be true to our principles, not follow such a plan.

During this analysis, we also came to believe in a principle more fundamental and thus more important than any plan: growth should come from success, but growth was *not* success. Put differently, did the company exist to reach a particular set of size targets on a particular timeframe? No. If the market opportunity for the company was small, so be it; the company would be small. If the market had room for a huge company of its type, so be it; the company would grow to be huge. In either case, what mattered was that the company did great work for its clients and was a great place to work for its staff.

> **growth should come from success, but growth was *not* success**

We did warn earlier that we kept coming back to this basic existence statement.

So we didn't create a business plan. More to the point, we rejected the idea entirely.

We started PT with no goals for its size; it would grow to be the size it earned by satisfying its clients.

We started PT with no plan for repaying its only investors—us.

None of this is to say, of course, that we didn't think

about what was possible. Of course we did. We had a strong sense that the market could support a business of our type that was large enough to be able to pay us and keep running. We didn't think we were starting a business that could be big, but we did figure in time it could hit at least a couple million dollars in annual revenue. (As was often the case, we were wrong. The company did so more quickly than we anticipated, and today it's many times bigger than that.) We were confident that the services we were going to offer would have real value for our clients. (We still are, and those services definitely do.) Those beliefs were enough for us to get rolling.

This approach, though, left us with the problem we cited earlier. Like any business, we needed capital to start.

We quickly decided to solve this problem in very old-fashioned ways, the same ways we noted earlier might be necessary for others starting a business: loans and sweat equity.

We determined from the very start that the company would ultimately pay its own way, so that no one, including us, ever had to focus on whether they were going to get a good return on the shares of the company they had purchased. In fact, the only shares of stock that exist to this day are the few we had to buy to start the company, and we spent only a token amount on those. Even though we were the only shareholders, we were not out to maximize shareholder value. We accepted that making the most possible money for ourselves was not only not our goal, it was a distraction from the business' reasons for existing.

This decision, which we have reaffirmed time and again, is one of the key reasons for the title of this book. We chose to limit our own greed—not because we're not sometimes as greedy as the next two people, and not because we don't like money (we do), but because greed was contrary to the reasons we chose to create the business. If you want to rethink the way businesses operate, you're going to have to confront this very basic issue, and not just once but many times. It will keep raising its head again and again.

So, we loaned the company a modest amount of money. These were real loans, with interest and contracts and all the standard terms of any loan. Unlike bank loans, however, we were not beholden to someone else's definition of credit worthiness or what we should do to repay them. As soon as we had enough cash in the bank to fund the company's operations and repay those loans, we did so—with the interest in the contract. Within the first few months of its existence, the company had repaid the loans and was operating on its own capital.

Sort of. It was operating on its own only because it had no employees, no office costs, and no benefits. Three of us worked from offices in our homes and for no salaries. For health care, we used either a spouse's benefits or COBRA coverage from a previous employer. It was old-fashioned sweat equity. We lived more modestly than in the past, and we survived on our savings. Soon, three other people were working varying amounts of time for us, but also with no immediate pay.

We kept track of the time all of us worked. We calculated what all of our salaries should be when the company could afford to pay salaries. (The two of us targeted salaries well below what we had made in larger organizations, on the assumption that one day our investment would pay off and because we were committed to trying to invent a new way to do business.) Though we didn't pay anyone any salary for most of the first year, we did carefully track what we owed each person and treated those amounts as debt the company would one day repay.

At the end of the first year, we wrote checks for what we could afford to all who had helped us, and we continued to track the remainder as debt.

In loaning the company money at standard interest rates, we accepted that we would not make as much back in the medium term as we might have gotten had we invested in something else. We were okay with that; we were willing to limit our greed for the good of the company.

In giving the company their time at no pay, our first colleagues were also betting that they would win in the end by helping create a place they would want to work. That bet paid off: all of them still work at PT.

Over the next couple of years, we paid off all the sweat equity debt, in effect paying all the original employees/time investors for the time they had given the company. We did have to loan the company money a couple more times for very short periods to deal with cash-flow issues, but each time the company repaid the loan quickly. We accumulated cash in the company, we took care of all involved, and soon enough the company had enough cash in the bank to float its operations and to pay everyone's salaries.

No business plan.

No external cash investors.

No targets for growth.

We saw no value in any of those.

What we did want, and what we focused on achieving, were our reasons for existence: doing great work for clients, and being a great place to work for our employees.

In those early days, we also continued to focus on examining all the standard assumptions of modern businesses. Those examinations led us to realize that if you're going to start a business, you should confront right at the start the central issue of how you're going to treat the owners (you) in relation to the employees (everyone else). The attitude you choose will say a lot about your business and its culture.

No business plan.

No external cash investors.

No targets for growth.

LIMIT YOUR GREED

CHAPTER 4

sense of egalitarianism

Though our backgrounds are fairly different, we share many fundamentally similar beliefs. One of the most important is our sense of egalitarianism.

We always hated working at places with different classes of employees. We never were very good at calling someone Dr. So-and-so, when Bruce was his name, or Director Such-and-so, when Betty was her name. People have intrinsic value and deserve respect because they are people, not because of their degrees, their job titles, the status of their families, the amount of money they have, or any other factor.

Fundamentally, we believe that companies should treat all people as having equal standing, regardless of their gender, age, race, religion, sexual orientation, or anything else.

An idea's merit, not the status of the person who offered it, should determine how a company values an opinion in making decisions.

Incorporating egalitarianism into a business is both fairly simple and extremely difficult. The simple part is making the decision to treat people that way. The difficult part is following through with that decision even when business needs and individuals' preferences push in contrary directions.

The practical consequences of this principle are significant.

It means, for example, that no task should be beneath anyone in the company, including us. If there is a spill in the kitchen, we can't just assume that someone "less important" than us will clean it up. This decision can be a challenge, because clearly there are people making less money than we are, so from a purely fiscal perspective, it would be better if they did the work. (Some people are also probably better at cleaning than we are.) Over time, a company is likely to hire people to run its facilities. Nonetheless, starting with a mindset of everyone being equal was critical to creating the kind of culture we wanted.

> An idea's merit, not the status of the person who offered it, should determine how a company values an opinion in making decisions.

Another consequence is that if we expected others to treat each other with respect, we had to treat them similarly. We don't claim we always get this right; we don't. When we make mistakes, however, we must own up to them and apologize. We end up doing that more often than we would like, though probably less than we should.

While we obviously hire folks for intelligence and

consider a degree from a good college a useful indicator, we are fine with hiring smart people who don't have college degrees. Ability, not credentials, matters most. This philosophy has helped us find some great people whom other places overlooked.

Of course, even when you want to treat all people equally, you have to face the reality that different people are better at particular tasks than others. A person who's great at writing computer programs might not be at all proficient in graphic design, or vice versa. Treating everyone with equal respect does not mean you can't focus different people on different jobs.

Similarly, market conditions and the value of each individual's contributions mean that not everyone should make the same salary. While everyone is equally valuable as a person, not everyone's time is equally valuable to helping the company serve its clients. For the most part, any business has to pay people what the market dictates. (More on that later.)

Even in cases in which market valuations made it possible for us to pay low wages to some of our staff, our existence statement reminded us that we wanted to be a great place to work. That desire meant that we needed to do our part to make sure that the wages of everyone in our company were such that they could afford to live within a reasonable distance of our offices.

Years after the company started, the heated debate about what the minimum wage should be made us realize that we had not given this area sufficient thought. We looked at local wages and at what we were paying, and we ultimately decided to raise the minimum amount we pay our lowest-paid employees so it was above anything those in our area were discussing as a new minimum wage. Even though we offered great benefits and were not having trouble finding entry-level employees, we were committed to being not just a good place to work for our people, but a great place.

To implement this change, we once again had to limit our greed by spending more than the business had to do to simply get by. We raised our entry-level salary, and then went back and adjusted upwards the salaries of all the people we had hired over the last year as if we had hired them at that new wage. Even if they were already making more than that minimum amount, we raised their pay to reflect where they would have been had we hired them at the new minimum.

As we've warned, limiting your greed and creating a new kind of company can cost you money—and not just in salaries. As we'll discuss later, being a great place to work comes from many different types of investments, not all of them monetary.

Egalitarianism proved to be an important founding principle for us, but it didn't cover every aspect of how the business should relate to its employees. To consider that subject more fully, you have to ask a question that few businesses seem to consider: what attitude will you take toward your employees?

CHAPTER 5

well-intentioned, responsible adults
who want to do good work

Ask the executives of almost any business how they feel about their employees, and you'll hear the same basic answers. They'll describe how important the employees are, how much the company values them, and so on.

Ask the same question of the employees, and you'll often get very different responses, because many businesses today have left their employees feeling unimportant, at risk, and constantly insecure. To make matters worse, Wall Street often rewards layoffs with increases in stock prices, which further hurts employee morale.

You have to dig deeper, though, than what either group says to discover what attitude the company broadcasts to its employees in its everyday actions. In a lot of organizations, the attitude feels adversarial, as if the companies see the employees as both people on their teams and individuals they must guard against.

If you want to create a new and different type of business, you need to decide in concrete terms the principles that will govern how that business should treat its employees. You can then use those principles, like the company's existence statement, to help guide all your other choices.

As we were thinking about how PT should work, we focused on what we had liked—and what we had disliked—about other places we had worked.

We liked being left to do our jobs.

We didn't like a ton of management.

We liked being trusted.

We expected oversight, but we expected to need it rarely.

We were very much self-starters, and we wanted to build a company of self-starters.

> **We believe employees are well-intentioned, responsible adults who want to do good work.**

After we'd hired a few people, we finally crafted a single sentence that summed up our attitudes toward our colleagues—and toward ourselves, because, after all, we are employees, too:

We believe employees are well-intentioned, responsible adults who want to do good work.

As with the existence statement, every bit of this sentence matters.

By "well-intentioned," we stated that we would assume that all our colleagues would have good intentions. With that assumption, we wouldn't have to worry about building safeguards against people of bad character, nor would we have to construct systems to make sure people weren't operating from hidden agendas. We assumed each person approached the company with good intentions.

The word "responsible" carries a lot of weight in this sentence. By it, we mean that people take responsibility for their work, for themselves, and for all their actions. We also use the word in the sense of people being reliable. Responsible people are people you can trust to do the tasks in front of them.

We also believe all of our colleagues are adults. They've graduated from childhood and don't need us or the company telling them how to run themselves. They are capable of analysis and complex decision-making that treat themselves, the company, and others intelligently.

The last clause of this attitude sentence is particularly vital, because when we say our colleagues "want to do good work," we mean exactly that. They don't do their jobs because anyone makes them; they do their jobs because they want to, because they have chosen as adults to enter into employment with the company, because this is work that engages them and motivates them.

By holding these beliefs about ourselves and all other employees, we eliminate the need for much of the management and other overhead of traditional organizations.

Nothing about people is ever simple, of course, and this belief is no exception. We learned quickly that it leads to certain challenges.

One of the most obvious is how to find people who truly are all that the business expects and needs them to be. We're discussing character here, not skill sets, and interviewing for character is never simple.

Initially, we addressed this issue by focusing our hiring on friends, family, and friends of friends and family—in other words, by choosing people about whom we had considerable knowledge. When a person's best references are people you know well and work with, you have a strong basis for trust. When we did run ads and recruited people we didn't know, we made sure to have multiple people interview the candidates, and we asked all the interviewers to focus heavily on character.

This approach served us well for a long time, but it also created its own issues.

The first problem to appear was that in a small company, people who were related in some way inevitably had to work together. When you have to comment on the work of a child, a spouse, or a close friend, you have to worry about your objectivity. We chose to have people recuse themselves from hiring and other financial decisions about those they were close to, and we stick to that practice to this day. Even so, occasionally people still find themselves in difficult situations. We have no easy answers here; we just involve multiple people and work extra hard to make sure all involved are acting objectively.

The other issue was equally obvious but took a bit longer to appear. As we'll discuss in the third part of the book, this emphasis on friends and family caused us to create a remarkably homogeneous group and thus a less diverse organization than we wanted. As more and more studies have shown, a diverse group with many different points of view tends to create better products and services, and we wanted to build the best possible team.

Despite having to deal with these challenges, we found that by truly believing this sentence, you can gain an amazing freedom, because it tells you not only how to treat people, but also and quite usefully what you don't need to do.

You don't, for example, need to police or monitor their web browsing, because they're well-intentioned adults, so they know how to behave responsibly.

You don't need to search them when they leave the building, because you trust them and they act with good intentions.

You certainly never need to treat them as the enemy, or as people to guard against, because you're all adults, and you're all operating from good intentions.

> **even people of good intentions may not know how best to behave in a complex situation**

None of this means, however, that you will never face tough employee situations; you will.

For example, even people of good intentions may not know how best to behave in a complex situation. We try to train people in the particulars of our business, but we know that all of us may at times encounter problems we weren't trained for. In those cases, we point to broader guidelines for behavior.

One of those is to suggest people look at the first word in the company's name: Principled. Does the behavior you're contemplating feel principled? Does it adhere to what you've learned about the way the company tries to behave? If so, you're probably ready to move ahead. If not, consider another alternative.

We also encourage people to ask themselves this question: if this conversation or decision-making process were to appear on the front page of *The New York Times*, would you be proud of how you appeared in the story? If not, it's time to consider another approach.

> **If this conversation were to appear on the front page of *The New York Times*, would you be proud of how you appeared in the story?**

Most of all, when in doubt, seek the counsel of others you trust, work with them, and see if you can reach a consensus.

Which an adult in any complex situation is likely to do anyway.

Our entire approach is, of course, inherently optimistic, because it doesn't address what happens when things go wrong. What are you to do, then, when you hire someone who turns out not to have these personal characteristics?

What if, for example, someone doesn't want to do good work and instead is just in their job to do the bare minimum and collect a paycheck?

After a lot of thought, we found ourselves with little original to offer here. Because we want to assume the best of people, when something goes wrong, we begin by trying to understand what happened. We try to help the person involved fix the problems at hand. This path can lead to more oversight, multiple conversations, and a slow rebuilding of trust—the typical HR process of dealing with issues. The goal remains to end up back where we started, with everyone behaving well.

It doesn't always work out. When it doesn't, you have to be willing to fire an employee. A single person violating the basic trust premises of an organization, particularly a smaller one, hurts the organization both by what that person doesn't accomplish and by making others carry that person's load. Similarly, a person who cannot do their job for whatever reason is not living up to their end of the deal with the company. We hate firing people, but as a last resort it is sometimes necessary. Our reliance on well-intentioned adults means that we cannot have someone who takes advantage of the company and its people.

With friends and relatives, we also considered in the hiring process whether we would be able to later fire that person if they did not work out. If we weren't willing to face that possibility, we shouldn't hire them.

If we were to be a great place to work, we had to treat

firing as a last resort, and we do. Long before turning to that option, we work hard with people to try to find good ways forward for them and for the company. When we can't, we fire that person as kindly as possible.

We try very hard to hire with care, and to fire with even greater care.

Our employee attitude statement has another problem: it is overly simplistic, because responsible adults of good will who start with the same data may still reach different conclusions. The only option when that happens is to work it out through open and honest conversation. With luck, the people involved will reach a consensus that works for all of them. If they can't, then we as the owners must get involved and, if necessary, make the final choice. As much as we like to avoid hierarchical decision-making processes, the need to make decisions at the speed of business will always be a reality, and sometimes you can't afford to wait for consensus (or even achieve it no matter how much time you have). We'll talk more about hierarchies and organizational structure in a bit.

A few words about our own decision-making process are relevant here. Though the two of us have worked together for a long time now (over 32 years as of the writing of this book), and though we agree on quite a few things, we are different people who approach many topics from very different perspectives. To pick but one simple example, to the best of our knowledge we have never voted for the same political candidate.

The standard way to settle disagreements between the owners in a company with two equal co-owners is the one our lawyers recommended when we were setting up the company: pick a third party to act as a tie-breaker.

We did not.

Despite lengthy arguments from our attorneys, we chose to have no official tie-breaking mechanism. We opted instead to trust that we would be able to work out our disagreements. We talk until we find a common ground. In the rare cases in which we fail to do that—they are rare, and when they happen the differences in our positions are inevitably small—the one of us who feels more passionately about his position typically carries the day.

> **We talk until we find a common ground.**

We believe all employees, including the two of us, are well-intentioned, responsible adults who want to do good work. That belief really does simplify matters.

Whatever you choose to believe about your employees, make certain the belief is clear to everyone, stick to it, and apply it to all the people in the organization.

Armed with the knowledge of why you exist, with a focus on treating all employees well, and with a clear and well-defined attitude toward your colleagues, you're ready to tackle the next question: how should you compensate them?

LIMIT YOUR GREED

CHAPTER 6

everybody wins, or nobody wins

That you have to pay people is a given businesses cannot avoid. You can rethink business all you want, but unless you're in the start-up stages and funding yourself via sweat equity, or you recruit only among those rich enough to do without a paycheck, you have to pay people to work. That's the easy part of the compensation discussion.

The more complex considerations arise when you start asking questions such as, will we pay at, above, or below market value? If we want to pay below market value, what inducement will we offer to persuade people to join a company that's paying them less than they can get elsewhere? If we're going to pay above market value, how will the business sustain that cost structure?

The most common answer, of course, is to pay market value, but even that choice avoids a question that is increasingly important in today's world of complex compensation packages: market value in what sense? Salaries alone? Salaries plus benefits? Salaries plus bonuses or stock options? If the latter, are those bonuses and/or stock options guaranteed or only possible? Anyone who's hired for a business or started one has had to address these issues. Companies end up coming at them from very different perspectives.

For us, the basic approach followed, as so many things did, from our existence statement: if we indeed existed to be a great place to work for our staff, we had to offer a great compensation package. We ultimately settled on paying salaries on par with or slightly above the market, because simply inflating salaries both raises your fixed costs and doesn't really address the entire compensation package. It also doesn't motivate people to make the company as a whole succeed. We wanted people to do well, but we didn't want to burden all of us with excessively high salaries.

One notion we found worthy of consideration was adjusting salaries to reflect performance and market value. If some people perform above their salaries, give them raises. If others deliver value well below their salaries, decrease their pay. Unfortunately, however reasonable this approach might sound, it's simply not workable, at least in the U.S., where people take on mortgages and other fixed expenses on the assumption that their salaries will either stay the same or go up.

if the company did well, who would win?

So, we started with competitive or better salaries, but we aimed to make the entire compensation package great. We wanted to make clear to all of us that we were signing up for a package, not just a salary, and we wanted to ensure that each employee would care about how well the company as a whole did.

At this point, we realized we had to ask one more

question, another obvious one but one we framed a bit differently than usual: if the company did well, who would win?

The traditional approach in tech companies is to give people stock options. If you are not out to maximize shareholder value, however, and if you don't have a clear exit strategy, then is stock, let alone stock options, even relevant? No exit plan means no way to turn stock into money.

More to the point, at least for us, was the question of whether we wanted other shareholders at all. We created PT as both a company and a social experiment, an attempt to do everything differently, so we did not want other shareholders or any focus at all on stock value. The focus should always be on doing great work for our clients and being a great place to work for all of us. We thus ruled out stock options, but we still had to figure out who would win, and how, if the company was doing well

This question boils down to whether the company will have multiple classes of people. We're not talking here the IRS-mandated groupings, such as part-time vs. full-time employees, nor are we discussing the fact that people with different backgrounds and skill sets earn different salaries. What we're focusing on is something most companies don't like to discuss: when it comes to compensation and other ways they treat people, they have different classes of people. Executives have better compensation packages than non-execs. People who go to work in office buildings every day often have different compensation packages than those working a shop floor. And so on.

We had worked at companies that took these differences farther than we thought was healthy. We'd seen a company lay off many people so that a small group of key employees could receive their very large bonuses—something many companies have done and are still doing.

We hated that approach. If you're really willing to limit your greed, can you accept good performers losing their jobs just so others can get bonuses? Even if you're the ones receiving those bonuses? We couldn't.

We also don't like the notion of classes, because it violates our egalitarian principles, so we wanted to avoid it as much as possible. Being willing to meet the requirement of paying market value for people meant accepting that people with certain skill sets were going to cost more than others, but we felt that was both reasonable and unavoidable.

> **Everybody wins, or nobody wins.**

Nothing in our principles or existence statement, however, said anything about being a great place to work for *some* employees; we wanted to be a great place to work for *all* of them.

The answer for us was ultimately simple: everybody wins, or nobody wins.

The mechanism for helping people win was equally easy to see: give them money. Given that we weren't going to offer stock or stock options, it was the only way we could see to reward everyone.

If everyone in the company is winning financially, it

means the company is making a profit. Some of that cash has to stay in the company, because the larger a business is, the more cash it needs to handle operating expenses and to get through lean times, but exactly how much depends a great deal on the nature of the business. For example, the vast majority of our expenses were predictable: employee costs. Had we been in the business of manufacturing physical products and needing to pay the costs of building inventory while we were selling those products, the answer would have been very different.

Profit sharing cash payments were clearly the way to go.

We settled on it early, and we still do it. We never count on it, and we encourage all employees not to count on it, because we can never guarantee how a year will go. We aim, though, to make profit sharing a part of each employee's overall compensation, so that when we as a company succeed, people earn not only market-rate salaries but also a piece of the profits.

One of the challenges of profit sharing is how to do it so that you motivate both higher- and lower-compensated staff members. Even a small percentage of the pay of someone who makes over a hundred grand a year can be a significant chunk of cash, but the same is not necessarily true for those who make far less. Percentages favor the highly compensated, while fixed-amount payments favor lower-compensated folks. Figuring out which will work best for your staff is vital.

Another challenge is the time between payments. You

can't know your profit with any certainty until your fiscal year is nearly over, which basically means you have to deliver profit-sharing payments on an annual basis. A year, however, is a long time to wait. More frequent payments can help with employee motivation and retention, but then you face a serious lack of knowledge when you're trying to decide on the earlier payments.

We ultimately decided to address these challenges by erring on the side of being generous to employees; after all, we want PT to be a great place to work. So, when the company can afford to do so, we provide both types of profit-sharing payments.

In good years, we make profit-sharing payments twice annually: in the mid-June paycheck (we pay twice monthly), and in the mid-December paycheck. The first payment reflects how the year has started financially and how we think the rest of the year is likely to go. It's a fixed-amount payment, so it favors the lower-compensated members of the staff. The second payment comes when we know how the year will end, so we know exactly what we can afford to share. It typically is a percentage of each employee's salary, so it favors the higher-compensated members of the staff.

By taking this approach, we share the profits on a regular cadence and try to balance how we reward both lower- and higher-compensated staffers.

What happens, though, when profits are low, or if the company fails to make a profit? We had to address that question, because both events were possible—and we have indeed encountered multiple lean years.

Our answer to handling bad times was the same as our answer to handling good times: we're all in it together, so we all win or lose together. We hope for good profit-sharing payments, but as we said earlier, we never guarantee them, because no one can guarantee they will make a profit. In tighter times, we all hunker down together. We've had years with minimal mid-year and end-of-year payments. We've even had years in which the only profit-sharing was a small, fixed-amount reward in December. In all our years, however, we've stuck to that basic principle.

Everybody wins, or nobody wins.

We also asked ourselves, what if the times were really bad? Would we lay off people if we had to, if doing so was the only way to keep the business alive?

Yes, we would.

We hated that answer, but we believed enough in what we were doing that if it came to that, we would do so. We'd first cut costs everywhere we could without jeopardizing our future; we might even reduce the salaries of some folks, such as us, who could afford to take that hit. Well before then, however, we'd do everything we could to make sure the company was financially strong and could delay such difficult outcomes as long as possible. (We'll talk more in a later chapter about some of the unusual ways we figured out to help the company be prepared for bad stretches.)

Fortunately, we have not had to do layoffs.

Once, late in our second year, we came very close. If we

didn't land a certain deal, even if we cut some salaries, we would not have had enough money for everyone. We had to talk to two recent hires, both friends of ours, and warn them that unless we landed that deal or something else very soon, we might not be able to pay them any longer. Fortunately, the necessary work came in, and their jobs were safe. Though that situation worked out, we had to accept that putting in place the principles to guide layoffs is important, should it come to that.

Everybody wins, or nobody wins. We're all in it together. These principles, we felt, should apply to a lot more than business, but we made sure we did apply them to our business. Whatever you do about compensation, consider carefully what it says about how you're treating your employees—all of them, not just certain groups.

We're all in it together.

In addition to these types of profit sharing, which apply to everyone, we also wanted to be able to tangibly reward those who went above and beyond the normal level of work for sustained periods. Giving a trophy or putting a name on a plaque is a nice thing, but we wanted to go beyond simple recognition. We ultimately created performance bonuses, which we award monthly and announce to the entire staff. In the spirit of making them reflect all the ways people can excel, employees can earn them by stepping up in a variety of different ways, including working lots of extra hours, learning new technologies, making big steps creatively, or taking on additional leadership challenges. The extra effort can't be just a long day or a hard week, though; it has to last all or at least most of a month. Similarly, the steps up in other areas have to be significant. Each performance bonus winner receives an additional thousand dollars (before taxes) in their next paycheck. A small group of people—a group that started as the two of us and has grown to be six people, six who have emerged as leaders—examine the work of the entire staff and award those bonuses. No one in the group is eligible for a performance bonus, but all (except us; we were never eligible) were frequent recipients previously.

Many companies have monetary award programs, but most also have a fixed award pool. Capping the awards certainly saves money, but it also puts top performers, sometimes those in very different areas, in competition in ways that don't tend to benefit them or the company. We chose instead to have no fixed limits on the number of recipients; it's possible to have none in a month (though we never have) or many (we've had nearly a quarter of the company win awards in particularly challenging months).

These awards benefit the company as well as the recipients, because by encouraging people to step up in temporary crunch times, they let the company avoid prematurely hiring additional staff. Put differently, the recipients win, but we also all win, because the company wins.

Over time, we faced one additional challenge: a group of key people, most of them leaders of the company, consistently performed at such high levels and were so vital to the company's success that we had to figure out how to reward them for this sustained effort. We did not want to introduce a new reward mechanism, so after much discussion, we ultimately settled on a mechanism that many companies have used: a modest profit-sharing multiplier. With this approach, these stars win a bit more than others in good times, but they, like us, remain tied to our central profit-sharing tenet: everybody wins, or nobody wins.

In this discussion of salaries and then profit sharing, we passed by a vital topic that deserves special consideration, because it's a place that can easily put principles to the test: how to handle raises.

CHAPTER 7

pay people what they're worth

Most businesses treat raises similarly—at least in the years when they actually award them. The typical policy is to pick a standard raise amount for good performance. They also provide rules that show how people might earn smaller or larger percentage increases. Most importantly, they supply fixed raise budgets to each organizational group, so that if one person gets an extra dollar, someone else has to lose that dollar.

We've never liked that system, and its many flaws go against our desire to be a great place to work.

For example, if everyone on a team is performing well, it forces the team's manager to penalize some good people to help others.

It also doesn't give the organization a good way to advance people who either joined the company at salaries below their market values or who proved over time to have more market value than their current salaries would indicate. Yes, you can sometimes use promoting those people as a way to give them more money, but then you frequently end up with title inflation.

Most of all, a fixed raise pool ignores the market reality that businesses frequently must hire people who don't have all the skills they need and then train those people in those skills. We decided early on that in addition to hiring for character, we would be willing to hire people, particularly junior staffers, who lacked skills specific to our business but demonstrated intelligence and a flexible mind, because they could then learn new skills rapidly. We would train those people in the skills we wanted. With the shortage of trained technical staff that the U.S. and many other countries now face, this approach is increasingly not only wise but necessary.

We started these people at low salaries, because their lack of relevant skills meant their market value to the company was low. As we trained them and they acquired new skills, their market value rose rapidly. If we gave them only the standard raise, their pay would quickly be way below their value. We hire smart people, so they would, of course, realize we were not paying them enough. We would in effect be training people so they were worth more, and then, by not giving them raises, encouraging them to quit so another company could benefit from the training we had done.

Not a good plan.

More importantly, treating people this way would most definitely not be making the company a great place to work. No, we wanted PT to be the kind of

> **When someone has to demand a raise and is right for doing so, the company has failed them.**

company that paid people what they were worth—without making them hold up the company for money. When someone has to demand a raise and is right for doing so, the company has failed them. (We have failed a few people over the years, but not many, and not often.)

As with so many areas, a basic principle—pay people what they're worth—became our guide.

Our raise practices begin traditionally enough: we choose a standard percentage late each year for the following year. We base that percentage on research into both inflation projections and IT industry salary increase norms. We share that research with the entire company, so everyone sees the facts on which we based our decisions. We then aim our standard raise for the following year a bit above the norm, because in all ways we want to make the company a great place to work. By default, employees who do good work earn the standard raise at the one-year anniversaries of their last salary changes.

At the same time, we regularly examine each employee's salary to make sure that what we're paying the person reflects their market value. Particularly with less experienced staffers, we watch for increases in skill sets that warrant increases in salary. When a person has grown their skill set and is now more valuable to the company, we reward that person with a raise that can be both earlier and larger than the standard. For example, when the standard raise was 4% at the one-year anniversary, we had multiple people earn 10% raises after only three or four months on the job.

The ideal result is a virtuous cycle in which employees deliver more value to the company, and the company rewards them with higher salaries. Of course, each increase in pay makes it harder for the person to keep growing in value to the company, because the person now has to add yet more skills, but doing so is always possible. Some individuals have gone multiple years with multiple and larger than normal raises.

Achieving such salary increases tends to be much harder for experienced people we hire from other companies, because we hire those people at market value into roles that are often similar to their past jobs, and their skill sets are typically well established. It's still possible for anyone, however, to increase their value to the company and to earn more frequent and/or larger raises as a result.

We have at times failed to notice as soon as we should have how well some people were doing. To make sure we don't repeat that mistake, we now track when we expect or hope someone will be ready for an early raise.

People increase their value. The company pays them more. They win by getting more money. The company wins by getting more value from them. Everybody wins.

Handling raises this way definitely increases the company's costs, but because the people who earn these raises are also increasing their capabilities, they can do more work—and often work for which you can charge more.

No discussion of raises or salaries would be complete without addressing the spread in compensation between the lowest- and highest-paid people in the organization. Though many different people have argued for all sorts of ranges, the extraordinarily high compensation of CEOs in many large enterprises continues to grab frequent headlines. As the heads of our company, we decided that this was another area in which we had to limit our greed, because if we were truly all going to be in it together, we should all move upward together in total compensation.

After doing some research, we ultimately settled on a theoretical compensation multiplier of sixteen, meaning that the total direct compensation (salaries + profit sharing + commission, if relevant) of the highest compensated full-time person in the company would never be more than sixteen times that of the lowest-paid full-time person. We focused only on full-time people, because we have rarely employed part-time workers.

> **the total compensation ... of the highest compensated full-time person in the company would never be more than 16 times that of the lowest-paid full-time person**

As it turns out, we've never come close to hitting this maximum, in part because we raised the minimum amount we pay anyone and in part because the salaries of our lowest-paid employees tend to rise quickly. Nonetheless, we believe that having some guideline in mind is both a good thing and a reminder that you should not err in favor of the highly compensated.

For business owners, this decision also provides one of the most profound and direct limits on your greed. It means that in extremely good years you have to share money you might otherwise have taken for yourself. We consider that an acceptable cost to pay for making sure everyone wins together, but it definitely can mean you take home less money.

We didn't say running a limit-your-greed company would be easy.

With an understanding of why your business exists, a clear stance toward colleagues, and your approaches to the key types of direct compensation in hand, one more compensation topic still remains open: benefits.

CHAPTER 8

great benefits

Benefits provide a way for a company to help its employees, recruit and retain them, and give them forms of compensation on which they don't, at least in the U.S., generally pay taxes. In tech businesses, providing at least decent benefits is a given, something you have to do if you want to recruit the best people. Those benefits definitely cost money, a lot of money, but you can't survive as a tech company without them. Companies in other industries, particularly those with many lower-compensated and part-time employees, often seem to go out of their way to avoid giving benefits.

If you want to be a great place to work, though, great benefits are a must.

The following details PT's benefits. They represent only one way to provide the sorts of benefits that help you recruit and retain the best employees. Each business has to find its own path.

When we started PT, as we mentioned earlier, we went for a time without any benefits. We used COBRA from a previous employer or a spouse's benefits for medical coverage. Soon enough, though, we had to face the topic of what benefits to give, what portion of their costs to charge employees, and so on. The news regularly reported on companies transferring more and more of the expense of their benefits to employees, because benefit costs, particularly in healthcare, were rising fast. Companies performed economic analyses of the pros and cons of benefits, and they priced the benefits according to the results of those analyses.

You can do that, and we at least considered it, but with PT's reason for existence including being a great place to work for our staff, we decided to approach the topic of benefits very differently. Instead of trying to minimize the cost of benefits to the company, we asked, what makes a benefits package great?

Search for "great benefits", and you'll get a huge variety of answers—over 700 million of them as of this writing. The answer seemed to us, however, to be simple: Great benefits above all else deliver the most value of the types employees want at the lowest possible price to them.

We started with the basics just about everyone needs and wants: medical and dental coverage. To give our benefits the greatest possible value, we went with the insurance provider with the broadest and deepest network in our state. To maximize the value, we went with the lowest deductible we could afford.

We then faced the issue of how much of the cost of each employee's benefits to charge to that employee. If we truly were out to have great benefits, the answer seemed clear: nothing. Zero is the lowest cost.

So we rolled out a medical and dental benefits package

with a low deductible and an extremely rare cost to the employee: nothing. At PT, you pay nothing for those coverages for you and your dependents.

As you might imagine, all of us at PT love these benefits, and this policy quickly became a recruiting aid. More importantly, it helped make PT a great place to work for our employees.

Each year, in the fall, we had to talk with our insurance agents and renew our benefits. As the company grew, the insurance provider raised our rates, typically by percentages well above the publicized national average increases for large businesses. As a small company, we had no ability to mount a meaningful protest to the increase. So, from a purely financial perspective, it would have made sense to pass along those increases to our staff.

> **Just because something is the norm doesn't mean it's right.**

We didn't. Just because something is the norm doesn't mean it's right. Great benefits helped make the company a great place to work, so we wanted to stick to them.

Instead of raising costs, we went back to our basic principles and asked, how could we make PT an even better place to work? This practice has become the norm for us: each year, when most companies are figuring out whether to make employees pay more for benefits, we instead consider how we could improve our benefits.

The result of engaging in this exercise for over a decade is a world-class benefits package that helps make PT a great place to work and one that delivers exceptional value to all of its employees.

For example, over time we moved our medical coverage to an HSA plan with a fairly high deductible. We did so, however, the PT way: the day you join the plan, PT fills your HSA card with the amount of the deductible for you (and your dependents, if any). So, as long as each employee stays within our provider's large and comprehensive network, the employee's total cost for both insurance and healthcare—services, drugs, everything—is typically zero.

Those benefits, though, are only the beginning of what PT provides to all employees.

> **The total amount each PT employee pays from each paycheck for benefits remains zero.**

We added the usual life insurance, short-term disability, long-term disability, and accidental death and dismemberment benefits, but again we did so at no cost to each employee.

To this day, the total amount each PT employee pays from each paycheck for benefits remains zero.

We were a small enough company that the SIMPLE IRA retirement plan was the right one for us, but when we instituted it, we once again considered how to make it great. We did the mandated corporate match of up to three percent of the employee's compensation, but we decided to have no vesting period. Instead, the matching funds go into each employee's account in less than a week after each paycheck, and the money is then theirs. We were not out to create handcuffs to keep people with us; we aimed to make a package that was great for them. Being a great place to work would be reason enough for people to stay at PT.

When the company grew large enough, we moved to a more traditional 401(k) program that allowed a corporate match of up to four percent of the employee's compensation. We still have no vesting period.

When we expanded the size of our facility, we built and equipped a small gym, so those who wanted to grab a workout at the office could do so. Both the company and the employees won on that one, because anything that makes it easy for you to stay at work is good for the company and saves you time.

When employees wanted the option of joining another gym or taking other types of physical training, we responded with a new gym benefit—this one taxable, per IRS regulations—of up to a hundred bucks a month. This benefit, though, gave us pause, because we'd been in companies with such benefits, and almost everyone took advantage of them to buy a gym membership—and then never went to the gym. We wanted to help people, not throw away money. Always keeping in mind our belief that employees are responsible adults, we made the reimbursement policy simple and sensible: if you go to the gym at least eight times a month, we'll reimburse you for up to a hundred dollars a month. We don't audit people to make sure they're really going; we trust them to tell the truth. As we told folks when we announced the benefit, if you're willing to lie to get this money, you should be ashamed. To the best of our knowledge, no one has ever bothered to lie about going to the gym just to get the money. (We did later drop the attendance requirement to four times a month to encourage more people to make physical fitness a priority in their lives.)

At benefits review time one year, as we were studying other leading benefits packages and considering how we could make ours better, we realized that a cafeteria would be a big win for both employees (they gain easy access to food) and the company (people stay in the building). We weren't a big enough company, however, to operate a cafeteria; we still aren't. Fortuitously, though, the first floor of our office building contains a small café that serves breakfast and lunch. We approached the owners, negotiated a deal with them, and created a new benefit: a quarterly allowance for food at that café. To pay for their meals, PT employees just write the amount on a sheet and initial next to it, and weekly the company pays the café the tab. This benefit was so popular that we ultimately doubled the quarterly allowance, so it's now $250 a quarter—enough to buy many but not all lunches for most folks.

In the same vein, we provide—and always have

provided—free coffee, tea, soda, and other beverages for all staff. Free refreshments save employees money, and they help us be more productive, because you only have to walk down the hall to get something to drink.

We learned time and again that if you really want to be a business that sticks to its principles, think about how everything you do affects your employees, and try to make the effects on them better.

Sometimes, that thinking will make you realize that what you were considering to be one thing could in fact be something far better.

For example, everyone in PT needs a laptop computer to do their work. That's typical in tech and indeed in most industries. The most common corporate policy is to offer people the option of choosing from a pre-approved list of computer models. This was an opportunity to turn a tool—the laptop into a benefit by letting all employees choose the laptop they want. (They also get to choose the large external monitor they want.) We made the benefit better by letting them do that every two years. People thus pick the tools they want to use, get to look forward to new tools on a regular basis, and are happier with both the tools and the company than they would be if we mandated specific makes and models. The company gains more productive employees, because those people are working with the tools they consider the best for their jobs. The cost increase to the company is real, but it's not huge.

During one tight period, to save money we delayed

laptop purchases, but a little over a year later, we reinstated the benefit. In this case, as in all matters, we all lived with the same rules.

Just as we have no laptop standards, we also have no standard office furnishings. The rule for each employee is simple: find a chair that works for you, and PT will pay for it. The same applies to furniture for offices.

When we started PT, we understood, as everyone in tech does, that the line between work life and personal life is increasingly blurry in many ways. If you're at work and need to do some shopping online, it's a rare company that will mind. If you need to leave early, perhaps to run an errand, most organizations support at least some notion of flextime and will have no problem with you doing so.

Most tech companies, however, also expect you to check your email from home at least once or twice an evening, and to be reachable when they need you. We certainly did. If we were going to have that expectation, however, it seemed only fair—and best for the employees—if we helped pay for the costs of doing those after-hours checks. So, at PT each employee gets to pick a new smartphone every two years, and we reimburse the monthly fee for the employee's phone. We also reimburse the monthly fee for each employee's home Internet connection.

All our benefits both help employees and help the company, which is ideal because then we're all winning, both as individuals and collectively as the company.

There's more, but at this point it's feeling like bragging,

and that's not our intent. The point is that if you want to reinvent your business, and if treating your employees well is truly not just a top priority but also one of the very reasons you exist, you can do a great deal more for them than you might expect.

One thing you can do for them deserves its own discussion: time off.

> **treating your employees well is truly not just a top priority but also one of the very reasons you exist**

LIMIT YOUR GREED

CHAPTER 9

unlimited vacation

Companies have been grappling for decades with how to deal with employee time off. Various types of plans have come and gone almost like fashion trends. For some years now, most companies with which we're familiar have chosen to take the same approach. They offer a total pool of paid time off days from which employees can take sick time, vacation time, or whatever other time off they need. Most employers in tech also seem to provide flexible schedules of some sort, so you can take off a few hours in the morning and make it up later that day, or perhaps later that week.

These days of potential time off also have been— and still are in many companies—a sort of currency that employees can save. Though there are always rules for when you have to use them or lose them, these times are essentially an asset that the company will have to pay you for should you quit. Companies in turn must do bookkeeping on this asset, reserve cash to cover possible payments for it, and so on.

Like so many aspects of modern business, this whole area feels like it has grown needlessly complex. Some of this complexity comes from the understandable and admirable goal of companies to be sure they treat everyone equally and fairly. Some of it, though, feels like it stems from a situation that has become almost adversarial, one that pits the natural desire of the companies for each person to work as much as possible against the equally natural desire of each employee to take as much time off as possible.

Over the past several years, many companies, particularly tech startups, have grabbed headlines by announcing "unlimited vacation" policies. These policies typically boil down to saying that there are no fixed limits on time off. Of course, no company can afford for all of its staff never to do any work, so practically speaking there really are limits on the amount of vacation time people can take.

We support this approach. It's a nice reinvention of the traditional rules. In fact, PT has operated with this type of policy since its beginning, way before we ever heard the term. We just had no name for it—and thus missed a marketing opportunity that other companies found. From our perspective, the most sensible time-off policy is a natural consequence of the principles of both wanting to make the company a great place to work and treating employees as responsible adults. At its core, the policy boils down to one simple statement:

Take off the time you need, but be sure to work it out in advance with those who are depending on you.

That's it. That's all we started with. From there, we would often outline all the things such a simple, trust-based policy implies:

No official holidays.

No vacation days.

No vacation assets to accrue.

No need to expend effort tracking time off. In fact, at our company no one tracks time off at all.

When we were small, this system worked without any other mechanisms of any sorts. On traditional business holidays, we worked if we were behind on projects, but otherwise our clients were off, so we took the time off. Each of us talked among ourselves before taking other time off, and we made sure the team could handle us being away.

Take off the time you need, but be sure to work it out in advance with those who are depending on you.

As the company grew, however, each employee was likely to be involved in many different projects (more on organizational strategies in a later chapter), so figuring out the ramifications of a person taking time off became more complicated.

We responded by creating a process—a very simple process, but, still, a process—for planning time off. We created an email list and populated it with the set of people who among them would have knowledge of all of the company's projects. To make sure your time away wouldn't hurt anyone, you'd email this list with your request, ideally after having first talked to the people you were working most closely with. If anyone on the list saw a potential conflict, they'd raise it. Otherwise, they'd say it was fine with them, you'd enter it on a shared employee time-off calendar, and off you'd go.

This process is still active today, and it's still working well.

We did, though, ultimately add one more layer of complexity about typical business holidays such as Labor Day: if it looked like the company as a whole could weather it, we'd email the entire staff and tell them to feel free to take off the day unless their projects required them to be at work. We referred to these days as "soft closes." In a services business that depends on frequent interactions with its clients, this approach made great sense for us, and it still works well.

In 2013, we took this holiday process further after we noted that over the week of Christmas and the following week, almost all of our clients were off work and expected we would also be off. We announced as a new benefit a soft close for those two weeks: if you were on a project that required you to work, then you worked, but otherwise you could take the time off. This really was the same thing as what we were doing with such holidays as Labor Day, but writ large. We ultimately decided to continue this process, because it had no obvious negative effects on our work and a very positive effect on most of our psyches. Some people did have to work, but relatively few, and even those folks did only what was necessary and otherwise took the time off.

In 2016, as part of our ongoing efforts to make the company a better place to work, we experimented with declaring a few days to be true work holidays, "hard closes." We're still analyzing how much doing so helped employees and whether it hurt the business. Constant reinvention should apply to this area, too.

To some degree, the fact that we never called our time-off policy "unlimited vacation" was poor marketing—and we are, quite correctly and like the other businesses that offer it, referring to the practice that way now that more people understand the term. Part of our resistance, though, comes from the simple truth that no company offers truly unlimited vacation. You can't sign your employment agreement and then take the next three years off. More to the point, though, this sort of policy actually has a dark side that we're still grappling with.

Many, many people take off less time than they might in other companies.

The main reason why is simple: they really are, as we have always believed, responsible adults who want to do good work. They don't want to let down their colleagues. They care about their jobs. They feel vested in the company and want it to succeed. All of these virtues are exactly what we hoped and believed people would bring to the company, but in many cases they came at the cost of some people simply not taking off much time. We're still contending with this issue and will touch on it again in the third part of the book.

So far, our entire focus has been inward, on the principles that directly affect the business and its employees.

No business, however, exists in isolation. Each business is a part of many different communities, from the cities in which it operates to the world. If you want to create a truly better business, you cannot ignore how the business relates to those communities.

From the beginning, we decided that a great business should always give back something, that while it existed to serve its clients and its employees, it must also accept that it has the same obligation to the world beyond its walls that all of us do: to help make that world a better place.

If you really are committed both to limiting your greed and to meeting that obligation, you have to figure out how you're going to make the business a good member of its communities.

a great business should always give back something

CHAPTER 10

what if everyone picked the charity list

When you're starting a small business, the company typically isn't in a position to give much to charity. Income is low, and profits, if any, are small. That was certainly the case for us. At the same time, we wanted to stay conscious of what we see as an obligation all of us share to help make the world a better place. We certainly hoped that each of our employees would be doing that in whatever ways they felt were appropriate, but we also wanted the company to give back to its communities in at least some small measure. Doing so seemed both socially important and entirely in keeping with the company's goals of limiting greed so that others could share in whatever wealth we might collectively create.

How to help the world was an open question.

If you want your business to remain true to its principles, you have to look at every area, even those as outside the daily flow of business as this one, with a fresh perspective that incorporates and reflects those principles. Many companies back particular charities, and that is a good thing. Would that approach, though, be in keeping with our fundamental thoughts about our company?

We decided it would not, at least if just we two picked the charities, because the company is everyone in it, not just some of its members.

The logical next question became, what if everyone picked the charity list? Then everyone would participate in the control (very egalitarian), and everyone's charities would have a chance to be on the list.

That felt right to us.

Implementing this simple notion, though, took a bit more thought.

The first problem was how to define a charity. We decided here to let the government do that for us: if an organization had earned the 501(c)(3) charity designation, we would consider it a charity.

Some organizations with a non-profit designation, however, worked in areas that involved involved political hot-button issues; the easiest examples are those groups that work on either side of the abortion debate. More generally, we did not want our charitable contributions to involve the company in such political debates, so we agreed not to support organizations involved in them.

We also faced the issue of whether we should place any other limitations on the charities. We realized then that we as founders specifically wanted to give back to the people in the company's local community—and, as we grew, in all the communities where we had employees—so we decided to focus on charities that helped local people.

We then had to decide how to fund this program. We could ask each person to donate, but that wouldn't be the company doing it. No, the money would have to come from the company. We decided to make these donations at the end of each year, when we would know how the company would finish the year and when many people are celebrating holidays.

We finally settled on these simple rules:

- Each employee gets to choose a charity that serves people in that employee's local area.
- Each charity must be a 501(c)(3) organization that does not exist primarily to support a political agenda.
- The company donates a small amount of money to that charity.
- If multiple people choose the same charity, the company will give that multiple of the donation amount to the charity.
- The company will select the base donation amount each year.

The goal here was never to put the company at risk, but rather to help within the company's means, so the gift-giving amount was modest. For the past multiple years, it's been $400 per employee. As the number of employees in the company has grown, so, too, has the total amount we contribute each year.

To speed the process, we've learned to keep a list of all previously approved charities and make it available to all employees.

The charities win by receiving these small donations, and the communities they serve—our local communities— win by the work the charities do. All of us win through the act of giving.

We've enjoyed a wonderful side effect of this program. Many of the charities send thank-you letters. We put those letters in a common area in our main facility, on a board and on a refrigerator, so everyone in the place can read them. We've heard more than a few people comment that walking by and seeing those letters makes them proud to be part of the company.

Doing good and making people happy by doing it: that's a beautiful thing.

This program, though, has one major limitation, one we imposed but a limitation nonetheless: it helps only locally.

Enter the TED conference.

All of us win through the act of giving.

CHAPTER 11

you get back more than you give

To be precise, enter the TEDActive conference.

We had both followed the TED conferences since Richard Saul Wurman created the first one in 1984. When Chris Anderson became TED's curator in 2001, he took it in new and exciting directions, a process he and his team continue to this day. In 2007, we decided to finally apply to attend TED—and we failed to get in for 2008. That year, however, TED started a satellite, simulcast conference, TED@Aspen, that ultimately became TEDActive, moved to Palm Springs, California and then to Whistler, Canada. TED@Aspen accepted us.

The experience in TED@Aspen was profound for both of us. It gave us a space in which we could take the time to think about issues far broader than our own concerns or those of our company. We've been going every year since then, though Mark missed one due to his mother's death. When the TED organizers decided to stop holding the TEDActive conference, they gave us the chance to attend the actual TED conference itself, and we took the opportunity. We've been going to the TED conference since then.

At one of the TEDActive conferences in Palm Springs, after a particularly moving talk, we realized that we wanted our company to do more, to help more, than it was already. TED addresses global issues, so we were particularly motivated to do good in the world at large.

We had also been discussing ways to make the company better for all of us employees, a topic we regularly pursue because, as we've noted many times, making the company a great place to work for its employees is one of the two reasons it exists. Some friends at another company were on sabbatical, so the topic of time off and sabbaticals came up.

Sabbaticals were a great concept. So, too, was the notion of making the world a better place.

How cool would it be if we fused the two?

On the spot, we outlined a new program that we then studied carefully, discussed with others in the company, and ultimately made our policy. This program has proven to help both employees and, at least in small measure, the world.

> **Sabbaticals were a great concept. So, too, was the notion of making the world a better place. How cool would it be if we fused the two?**

At PT, each employee is eligible for a seven-week, paid sabbatical every seven years. If for one week of that seven you will work at a charity, PT will give five thousand dollars toward your travel expenses to go to the charity. If your travel expenses are under five thousand, PT will give the rest—or even the full amount—to the charity itself.

You get seven weeks off. A charity somewhere in the world gets a week of time and probably some cash. It costs you only your time.

Everyone in the company loved the program. Everyone we've ever told about the concept seems to love it.

We had to work out a lot of details, of course. We ultimately decided that to protect the rest of the people covering for you while you're out, you can't add more time or break the time into smaller chunks; it's a fixed, contiguous seven weeks. You don't have to take it in your seventh year; you can take it whenever works out for you and the company. Like all other time off, you have to make sure the people you work with can cover for your absence. We use the same time-off email list we mentioned earlier, but in this case, we do ask for at least three months of notice so your teams can plan how to handle your absence.

The charity must conform to the same basic guidelines as the local charities, but it can be anywhere in the world. In keeping with our faith that employees are responsible adults, the charity work is optional, not mandatory. We hope you'll do it, but we don't require it.

The one thing we did mandate was that while on sabbatical, you go completely offline from the company. We wanted sabbaticals to be times in which employees could truly clear their heads, detox from stress, and just take a break. When you go on sabbatical, you post an out-of-office message and don't interact with the company again until your first day back.

We announced the policy, heard great reactions, and waited for the first sabbaticals.

We learned that though most people would indeed give a week to a charity, a few did not. We were frankly saddened by that fact, but we had to accept it.

Those who have taken sabbaticals and done charity work have given time to organizations both local and far away. We've had people work in Bolivia, Portugal, Italy, Cambodia, and southern Africa, to name but a few. We've had others work locally. For some, the five thousand dollars covered travel expenses, with the rest going to the charity. Some who could afford it paid their own expenses and had PT donate the full amount to the charity. The charities of those who worked locally also received the full five thousand.

In talking with each of the people right after their sabbaticals, we learned that the time away was indeed cleansing, and that everyone felt vastly better for having done it. From the many folks who've done charity work on their sabbaticals, we came to understand something very important, a lesson we also learned from our own charity work: you get back more than you give.

You can't know in advance exactly how the charity work will touch you, but in every case so far, it has affected people profoundly and made them feel better. It's given them more than it cost them.

We also learned that the moment of return from sabbatical is a great time to re-examine what each person is doing in the company and wants to be doing in the future. Most people do return to their roles, but not all; sometimes we collectively find that new or at least slightly different roles will better serve both the person and the company. That discussion is another benefit of sabbaticals.

After a few folks had taken sabbaticals, we decided to try to do more for the charities they chose by making a video about each person's sabbatical. Our studio team creates the videos, we get the charities to okay them, and then we let the charities use them for no cost. We also post those videos on our YouTube channel; you can easily find and watch them.

Even relatively new policies, such as our sabbaticals, benefit from regular examination and reevaluation.

Sabbaticals, particularly our version of them, definitely also cost the company. Five thousand dollars per person is not a small amount, but it's small compared to the cost of losing a person for seven weeks while still paying their full salary. If everyone stays with PT long enough to take a sabbatical, the program will run about two percent of our base salary costs. (It's the equivalent of one week off a year.) You also have to make sure you have enough people to cover for the steady stream of sabbaticals.

In our judgment, though, the benefits far outweigh the costs. With sabbaticals, in a sense broader than just the company, everybody wins.

We've talked a great deal so far about how a company

can relate to its customers, its staff, and the world, but we have not yet gotten down to the vital topics of exactly how you can align your business' operations with your principles. Reinventing business principles is one sort of challenge; finding the right ways to implement those principles is a very different task.

One of the first and most important decisions you have to make is how to structure your organization. You could do the usual thing and start drawing org charts and filling them with the types of people you'll need—but that would hardly be rethinking how businesses should work, would it?

No. Instead, you're now ready for the first step in rethinking how your business should operate: (re)inventing your business' structure.

PART TWO

Reinvention

LIMIT YOUR GREED

CHAPTER 12

no org charts and no titles

Businesses love org charts as much as bears love honey. The amount of human energy that goes into creating and updating org charts could power a large city for years. This isn't irrational, because the way a business structures itself matters. It affects everything from how people gauge their place in an organization to how the business interacts with its customers and its suppliers.

Org charts are also by design limiting. They tell people what to work on—and by logical extension, what not to do. They assign responsibilities and authority—and they limit both.

We thought a great deal about org charts in the early years of PT. Initially, they didn't matter, because we had no employees, but we knew the day would come when we would need to worry about the organization's structure. We considered all the places we'd worked and what we'd liked and disliked about each.

About the same time, we both also read two very interesting and provocative books by Ricardo Semler: *Maverick*, which tells the story of how he rebuilt his business, and *The Seven-Day Weekend*, which examines the blurring lines between work life and home life. In *Maverick*, Semler discusses how he eliminated many levels of management and let people organize themselves, and how well that change ended up working. We stirred that with our fundamental attitudes toward employees and our own dislike of being managed, and we came to an interesting conclusion.

We didn't want to have an org chart.

We also didn't want to have any titles. (On our articles of incorporation, we had to assign some titles to each of us, but we decided those titles existed only for that paperwork and would not matter in our day-to-day operations.)

> **Titles, like org charts, tend to box in people and to limit both what they do and what they think they can do.**

Titles, like org charts, tend to box in people and to limit both what they do and what they think they can do. We didn't want to limit people and their possibilities to a box on a chart. We didn't want anyone, most especially us, to consider any task beneath him or her. We didn't want an org chart to undermine our egalitarian principles.

On our internal employee contact database, people are free to fill in their own titles, though we don't use them in any official way. The attitude with which most people have treated those titles has only served to reinforce how unnecessary they are. Some of our favorites have been Tiny

Tyrant, Señor Techie, Lesser Peon, Chief Sleep Officer, Volunteer Extraordinaire, Tinker, Visualizer, and Village Idiot.

So, PT began with no org chart and no titles.

Nearly fifteen years later, and now with going on ninety people, it still has neither.

Once you abandon org charts and titles, you find that you have to reinvent a great deal about how the business works. You can't rely on traditional structures, so you must rethink your processes.

This is a good thing.

You certainly don't want everyone to work on everything; that ignores their expertise and the skill sets for which you hired them. On the other hand, if people can contribute in areas than their primary ones, you may well want to take advantage of those contributions. So, you need to make sure you remain flexible and able to tap the various types of expertise of everyone in the company.

Org charts frequently affect, if not determine, the amount of time people spend on a project. In a typical company, if a project hits your team, your team has to handle it or, if it cannot, petition other teams for help.

What if instead the project hits the whole company, and you have the expertise of all of the company's employees to draw upon? People with particular skill sets can contribute to the project for as long as you need them, and then they can move on. Clients win by having more expertise available to their projects. Employees win by getting to work on a wider range of activities.

The lack of an org chart also emphasizes how much everyone needs to work together. You might be leading one project and getting help from a colleague on that project, so your colleague is more or less working for you on that effort. At the same time, though, your colleague might be leading a different project and using you for your expertise on that one, so you are more or less working for your colleague there. Relationships can be fluid and reflect not a single fixed structure but rather the needs of the work, which means the needs of the clients. This constant focus on serving the clients well meshes perfectly with our existence statement.

Org charts also affect how information flows, with most data moving laterally only within the local branch of the organizational tree. Remove those limitations, and data can flow to all the people who need it. People who need to talk can do so without worrying about whether they're crossing artificial structural lines.

We have encountered some minor hassles with not using titles. For example, some of our clients really want us to have titles, especially if we need to sign paperwork. In that case, we use something appropriate. Sometimes, the right title can open doors, so we personally might use something like Co-founder when necessary. Using titles, however, is the exception, not the norm.

Despite the minor hassles for some clients, this approach has proven to deliver great value for them. As we mentioned, PT is a service business and a sort of consultancy. In PT's early days, virtually all projects involved product testing. In competing firms, if a testing job required six person-weeks of effort and had to finish in three calendar weeks, the team on the job would typically be two people. The client would get the benefits of what those two people knew, but it also would have to live with their limitations.

As we grew, we found that in our model the same project frequently involved 15 or more people, each applying his or her expertise in just the amount the project required and then moving on. The client gained the value of the experience of all those people, so each project benefitted from a much broader range of expertise and perspectives than would normally be possible.

It was immediately apparent that each project needed an organizer, someone to stick with it from start to finish and provide a single contact point for the project's client. We learned, though, that the amount of time a project's organizer (or "lead") would need to spend on that project varied widely. Sometimes they would need to be a strong individual contributor on the project, but at other times they would act primarily as a coordinator.

In an organization without a formal structure, though, who would appoint those organizers, those project leads?

Two different answers appeared.

The first was what we had hoped for: leaders emerged through the wisdom of all the employees. People chose to look to certain individuals for guidance, and with each success those people became more obviously leaders. Different people were leaders in different areas, but their work quality and leadership skills led others to follow them. We had hoped for a meritocracy, and in large measure one grew on its own. In some companies, people who are better at politics than at doing work can go a long way, because they can successfully manipulate a small group of decision makers above them. When those same people have to convince a large group of their colleagues to follow them, however, it's a different story.

> **You'll know you're a leader when people are following you.**

Those new to PT will sometimes ask, "How will people know I'm a leader?" They're seeking someone to appoint them as leaders. They want someone to impose them on a team. At the risk of sounding a bit too flip, the correct answer is, "You'll know you're a leader when people are following you." Over time, more and more people have emerged as leaders in various ways and in a broad variety of areas of expertise.

The second answer to how to identify leads was both obvious and yet somewhat behind the scenes in day-to-day operations: the two of us could and sometimes did designate them. Even though PT was a company without an org chart or titles, it still contained two people—the owners, the two of us—who by their ownership had more ability to affect things, and thus more organizational power, than everyone else. Though we, too, might at times be leads and at other times act as individual contributors, our status as owners remained special. So, we acted as the court of last resort and designated leads when necessary.

More generally, our structure-free company always had the option of checking with the owners. This was both a feature, in that it worked, and a bug, in that we relied on it for too long. More on that in the third part of the book.

Over time, we came to understand that the way the company approached projects was a bit organic, a creature reorganizing itself to fit the challenges in front of it. We've at times called it a recombinant organization, and in many ways that's an accurate summary, though of course some parts, such as the two of us acting as owners, did not change.

This freedom from org charts turns out to yield additional advantages, both for each individual employee and for the company as a whole.

LIMIT YOUR GREED

CHAPTER 13

one person's boring job is another person's challenge

A great benefit PT derives from the lack of org charts and titles is that the company naturally utilizes dynamic teams on projects. As we mentioned in the last chapter, rather than dedicating a few people to a short project and having them handle all aspects of it, we commonly use as many as 15 or more people on a project. This way, the client gets the best possible expertise in each relevant area, and both newer and more established employees gain the opportunity to face new challenges. The clients win, all of the people involved win, and so does the business.

Everybody wins—a common theme and a good one.

This emphasis on spreading tasks and knowledge throughout the organization turned out to produce three more benefits for the company.

First, it motivated us to constantly focus on teaching new skills to people. In our experience, one person's boring job is another person's challenge. If more senior people have done a task so many times that they're bored with it, they are motivated to train more junior people to do the same task well. If those same people want to go on vacation and not get a call for help from a confused colleague, they are motivated to spread around their expertise and train their colleagues. The senior people still work responsibly, of course, because under our key assumption about employees, all the people on a project act as responsible adults.

The more experienced folks win by training the newer folks, because they to spend their time on more complex work that's more challenging and interesting to them. Those more junior people also win, because they add skills and acquire a broader range of expertise. The business as a whole wins, of course, by having a deep reservoir of individuals with key skills and thus fewer single points of failure.

A second good by-product of this system and of the generally dynamic nature of the company is that it helps us easily identify people who need more training. When leaders are seeking people to work on their projects and no one asks for a junior employee, that person probably needs more training. The collective wisdom of the staff also identifies those whom the company needs to help improve.

The final benefit ultimately is cost. The desire of all employees to seek new knowledge and do better work leads to training, which in turn leads to the work finding the lowest cost path to doing the job well. It's in no one's interest for any project to fail, but everyone—the clients and those in the company—wins when a project costs less to execute. The more senior (and expensive) people still provide oversight and check the quality of the work, but over time the more junior (and cheaper) folks gain those skills and no longer need as much training or supervision.

Thus, instead of having to target particular employees

at particular types of jobs and then always having to figure out how to provide growth paths for them, the company's very lack of structure lands people in job types for a while, and then moves them to other types.

This natural growth of people also leads to cross training. People learn not only what they are currently working on, but what they may be working on in the future. The mix of people learning a new skill and those who still know that skill—but no longer regularly use it—allows for flexibility when unexpected work comes in, when people take vacations, medical or parental leave, or sabbaticals, and even with the inevitable turnover of employees. (Our turnover has proven to be low, but it is not zero.) As people learn more, they can do more valuable work—and, as we noted earlier, consequently be worth more in the market and thus get more pay from the company.

This approach is not without its drawbacks, of course. Two reared their heads early and continue to this day. (Others arose only as we grew; more on them in the third part of the book.)

The first may sound foolish but proves to be more of a challenge than you might think: explaining to clients how the company works. A small company that is intensely focused on doing great work for its clients—that, in fact, exists to do that—seems at odds with what can sound like a hippy-dippy approach to organization. When clients want to know exactly how many person-hours at each hourly rate we are allocating to a project, they are asking a question that makes great sense at most consultancies—but not at PT. We don't approach projects at all that way. We don't account for time that way. We estimate project costs based on our experience, and then we let the team build itself according to the project's needs. We almost never know in advance exactly all the people who will work on a project. It's easy to sound like you're dodging the question when you give that sort of answer, but at PT, it is simply the truth. If you choose an unusual organization structure, you can expect it will concern or confuse at least some of your clients.

> we let the team build itself according to the project's needs

The second is a challenge that this lack of structure creates for many people inside the company: integrating new hires. For most people new to PT, nothing is more confusing than the way we approach projects. Some junior people take to it quickly, particularly if they have no prior experience in business, because they have no habits to break. Most senior people, on the other hand, require a significant period of adjustment, typically at least six months and sometimes as long as eighteen months, even two years, before they find the rhythm of projects and feel comfortable with them.

This problem is often particularly acute with people you hire with the hope that they will one day be leaders. When one such person seemed ready to lead their first project and stepped into that role, they immediately asked, "What is my staff, and what are my resources?" In any normal organization, those questions make sense and are necessary. In one without an org chart, however, they make almost no sense. Those who understood the PT system responded, "What expertise and resources do you need for the project?" The newcomer was looking to fit the project to what the company gave them; those with experience understood that the company as a whole had to provide whatever the project required. If you're not careful, some who are new to the company will quickly become frustrated, even convinced that you're hiding something from them. The truth is that the shift in how you have to look at projects is so great that some people have trouble making it for quite some time.

If you manage to implement a flexible or alternative structure, such as the one PT uses, you will also end up facing another challenge: how to facilitate the work and communications styles the structure needs to thrive.

LIMIT YOUR GREED

CHAPTER 14

learning this communication style

Working and communicating in any unusual organization can be tricky, particularly if you've come from one in which you communicate primarily up and down an org chart. Though learning our new communication style can be difficult for some, over time it leads to a faster, more knowledgeable organization.

If you're considering setting up an unusual organization, we've found a few communication and work guidelines to be helpful.

When in doubt, tell all the people involved. People can always opt out of discussions if they so choose. This is particularly easy in an email-centric and instant-messaging (we use Slack) culture like ours. When in doubt, add the person to the cc list or include them on the Slack channel.

Be clear, direct, and concise. The harder you make it for people to understand what you mean, the more time you'll end up spending on the discussion. In emails and Slack messages, this means using simple declarative statements where possible and clearly indicating questions or requests near the beginning of a message rather than burying those items deep within it. It also means giving credit where credit is due and taking blame when you're at fault. Passive voice is the enemy of clear communication. Rather than hide who did what, state it directly. For example, rather than using passive voice to say, "It was decided," opt for the more direct and clear active-voice statement, "Cindy and Bob decided."

The company's culture then must reward that behavior by accepting the information and using it to make smart decisions—and not to beat up those who made a mistake.

Respect the time of all involved by staying on topic. While amusing anecdotes and pet peeves have their places, productive meetings, email threads, and Slack channels are not those places.

Do not play games. Be as direct as possible. The goal of communication should be to inform and, where appropriate, to convince, not to wheedle or jockey for position.

Write messages and conduct meetings with an eye toward minimizing the cost to all involved. Each person should be aware of the audience of each communication and make the communication as easy to process for that audience as possible.

Don't try to cram too much into a single meeting or message. If you ask too many questions, odds are good that the recipients won't answer them all—and some of the readers of the message won't remember all the answers.

Choose the right communication method for the situation. Email threads with a large cc list or Slack channels can be great for informing all the people involved in a project of the project's current status. They typically serve less well for hammering out the best way to solve a particular problem.

A face-to-face meeting or a video or phone call will often lead more quickly to a resolution.

Our lack of formal structure also led us to have to figure out the best ways to resolve conflicts. When the goal of a discussion is to settle a disagreement, an org chart can provide an easy path forward. In a typical organization, when two people can't agree, or two teams can't agree, they can march up the org chart until they find a point of intersection and turn to that person for arbitration. In a company without such a structure, conflict resolution instead becomes a communication task for all the people involved.

For example, if three different leaders are asking for an individual's time on three different projects, that person either has to accommodate all three requests or, if that isn't possible, get those three leaders together and ask them to work it out. Why does that responsibility fall to each person? Because each and every person is a responsible adult who wants to do good work, which in part means wanting all three projects to succeed.

Were those involved unable to come to a resolution that works for all involved, as we mentioned earlier, they had to escalate to the owners—us. One or both of us was almost always available to arbitrate, but fortunately such conflicts proved to be the exception, not the norm. Even so, in such cases we again

you can grow a successful business with unusual structures

became a bottleneck—another aspect of the challenge of letting go that we discuss more in the third part of the book.

Though problems do arise, our experience suggests strongly that you can grow a successful business with unusual structures, even one that is constantly reforming itself and never has an org chart, if you are willing to invest the necessary time and training in communication. We believe the result is worth the cost, because both the organization and the individuals become stronger for having to learn how to adapt to changing needs.

If you're going to embrace open communication, you'll have to be ready to explain your choices, including your investment choices, such as hiring. If you're rewarding people with profit sharing, everyone should realize that each investment has the potential to be money from all pockets, including theirs.

Even in a business with very open communication, handling the financial aspects of the business can be tricky. You have to be willing to share how the business manages its money, handles spending, and so on. At the same time, you must manage your finances well; any business that doesn't pay close attention to its financial health does so at its peril. Surely this is one area in which business norms must prevail.

Yes and no.

Before you dive into financial operational controls, however, you should consider exactly how much financial data you're willing to share.

CHAPTER 15

transparency is a bedrock

Most people in most businesses do their jobs with only a minimal understanding of the company's financial situation. Some of that feels natural, because the work most people do does not involve a regular scrutiny of the company's finances. Some of that lack of understanding, however, often feels as if it's coming from a conscious decision on the part of upper management to keep a great deal of financial data private. If the company is public, the situation is even more complicated, because many laws govern what a company can disclose, when, and to whom. Such companies legally must manage the disclosure of most of their financial data very carefully.

We had (and have) no plans to go public, so we didn't have to worry about dealing with that particular set of problems. In the beginning, when only the three of us worked at PT, two of us were owners and one managed the finances (and the office and many other things), so we all knew all there was to know about our money. As we grew, we had to decide what to disclose, and how, and when, and to whom.

When you consider our core belief that employees are well-intentioned responsible adults, it seems obvious that we should be completely transparent about our finances. If indeed we hold that belief, and if we are all in it together, with everybody winning or nobody winning, then why wouldn't we tell everyone in the staff how we were doing financially?

We could see no reason at all, so we set out to do just that.

At that point, we ran into a few interesting realities.

The first was the one we mentioned above: we all had jobs to do. The details of a company's finances are constantly shifting, as it pays people, makes sales, spends money to buy things, receives payments, and so on. Updating everyone on each change would simply cost too much staff time and attention—and few would even want the data.

The other reality surprised us a little (though not a lot). If you're going to tell people everything about your finances, you're going to have to tell them about salaries—particularly in a company in which the vast majority of the expenses are people-related costs. One day when we were about twelve people, we all gathered around our single conference table, and we posed a question to the group: how would you feel about all salaries being visible to all employees? Both of us were generally in favor of the idea, as were a couple of others, but the overall reaction in the room was strong and clear: they did not want to share this data. They *really* didn't want to share this data.

So we don't. Salaries and related individual compensation information (benefits, commissions, profit sharing), which collectively compose our biggest single expense item, remain private. Sharing that information proved to be a step too far for our folks, and we expect that if we gave the same survey today to our much larger company, people would respond the same way. Even if only a vocal minority wanted their compensation to be private, though, we'd feel obliged to keep that information confidential.

The rest of the financial data, though, everyone agreed was fine to share.

So we do. Financial transparency is a bedrock of the company. More generally, transparency in as many areas as possible is a key goal of ours. If you work on a project, you know how much revenue is associated with that project. The same goes for direct expenses for the project, and for current opportunities with clients. If you want to know what we spent on an item for a project, you can ask the people who manage the company's money, and they'll tell you.

If you want true transparency, though, you must do more than simply make such data available. One of the best ways to hide information is to declare it available but make sure everyone is so busy that no one really has time to ask for it. We didn't want that to happen. So, each month we share with the whole company what new projects we landed, what opportunities we are pursuing, and so on. We talk about how the future looks. We take questions. We want everyone to know how the company is doing.

In addition, we try to annually show the whole company where all of its money is going. Dominating the expense charts are, as we've noted, the costs for our staff, but we also show the other areas in which we're spending money.

You might notice that despite our stated desire not to make maximizing our profit the main goal, and despite our refusal to craft a business plan, we just mentioned sales goals, current and past performance, and other financial standards. So, we do care about money, right?

You bet.

We never said we didn't. We've always wanted to make a good living, and we are fiscally extremely conservative. We manage our money very carefully—more on that in the next chapter—and we highly recommend that any business—and indeed any person—do the same. We just don't make profit the number one goal.

So, the answer to what we share is everything except salary-related information, and the answer to whom we share it with is everyone in the company. That leaves the question of how to share it.

That question immediately begs an even broader one: how, in general, do you want to share relevant news with your company? All-company emails are easy enough and certainly appropriate for some things, but they aren't great for holding conversations, or for topics that require complex explanations.

We've long been big fans of short, all-hands meetings, so for us they were the obvious answer. Such meetings are clearly expensive, because you're tying up everyone in the company in a non-revenue-producing activity, but if you keep them brief and on point, they can be incredibly helpful tools. We decided to make them a regular feature of PT, so every month we hold an all-hands meeting, with remote employees joining via conferencing software. We discuss the financial updates and other news, and we invite questions. (We also provide lunch—typically pizza and salad—for all the local staff.) The goal is both to share information and to cultivate a culture of transparency and open communication. (In the third part of the book, we'll discuss some additional ways we learned we had to approach those same goals.)

Financial transparency is a good thing and relatively easy to achieve. Controlling your finances in an open and low-structure environment, however, is a much more complex topic. You might, for example, know exactly how much money the company has, but if you want to spend some of it, what must you do?

> **Financial transparency is a good thing and relatively easy to achieve.**

This topic put our principles to the test like no other, because as we said earlier, we are fiscally conservative, and we wanted to manage the company's finances tightly. Trying to resolve the conflict between transparency and tight control proved to be initially challenging—and has only gotten more so over time.

LIMIT YOUR GREED

CHAPTER 16

each financial control comes with its own costs

Sharing financial information with everyone is simple. Sharing the checkbook with everyone is something entirely different, an act that would put all the assets of the company at each individual employee's disposal. Just how much spending authority you give each person in a company is a very important question, because in the most fundamental way the ability to write a check is also the ability to get the company in a great deal of trouble.

When you couple that risk with our core belief that employees are well-intentioned responsible adults, you find yourself in very tricky territory.

Most businesses don't face this problem. They address financial control in the same basic ways. A central group watches over the money and has sub-groups that handle things like purchasing and paying bills. Automated systems help track expenditures. At regular intervals, the organization trues up its books so it knows where it stands.

From an operational perspective, managers at various levels throughout the organization receive budgets of different sizes from some sort of central budgeting authority, one whose final decisions the CEO typically must bless. Each manager has a sign-off limit, with the limits being higher as you go higher in the org chart.

People at all levels prepare budgets for the upcoming year, typically in the fall, and then go through a long budget review cycle. The company often makes people review budgets frequently, at least quarterly, sometimes more often. The ability to control budgets becomes one of the most prized abilities in many companies, and the amount of human energy that goes into budget fights is enormous.

Worse, most people quickly learn one of the bad lessons of budgets: spend it or lose it. A budget thus becomes both a forecast of what a group will need to spend and a requirement to spend (at least) that much within the time period the budget covers.

> **the area of financial controls is one clearly ripe for reinvention**

Not a single thing about this system sounds optimal.

All the components are understandable, and each probably arose for good reasons, but the whole contraption is at least rickety, if not downright broken.

Put differently, the area of financial controls is one clearly ripe for reinvention.

Contemplating how to reinvent them led us to confront the harsh reality we mentioned above: in facing this challenge, we have two competing sets of desires and principles.

On the one hand, as we've explained, PT is all about

treating employees as responsible adults, about being as egalitarian as possible, and about transparency. Those beliefs argue strongly for little to no financial control. Trust is at the company's core, so we should trust people to spend wisely.

On the other hand, as fiscal conservatives we wanted to run a very tight fiscal ship, spending what we needed but no more. We wanted to travel as lightly as possible—more on that in a future chapter—and amass as few possessions as we reasonably could. We wanted to start lean, stay lean, and run lean. If we were going to spend money, we wanted to do so when it helped us either do great work for our clients or be a great place to work for our employees.

To resolve this conflict, we considered first how the two of us would spend the company's money. We did so carefully, because in the early days of a small company, money is scarce, and consequently every expenditure counts a great deal. We spent only after discussion, because we wanted to make sure both of us were on board with any expenses. As you'd expect, we devoted more thought and conversation to larger, continuing expenses (e.g., hiring people, taking on more space and thus increasing our rent) than to smaller, one-time costs. (Some of these, such as deciding to have the company reimburse the fifteen-buck cost of a lunch meeting at a Chinese food joint in a nearby outlet mall, required only a single, overarching decision).

One thing we didn't do was create budgets. We spent money when we agreed we should do so, when the business needed it, but not otherwise. We didn't allocate ourselves—or anyone—pots of money to spend. No one should spend a company's money simply because they have some of it sitting in a pot. Instead, each expenditure should be toward a business goal. For us, the business' needs, not the existence of a budget, always drove spending.

We thus had developed two guiding principles: expenditures should come after discussion, and budgets were not in general a good thing.

We mentioned sales goals earlier, so it's worth noting that we determined our sales goals—the flip side of the expense equation—in much the same way as we managed expenses. We looked at what we had already committed to spend, which we see as very different from a budget. This list included first and foremost the costs of our current staff and then also covered such commitments as rent, bandwidth, and so on. We then factored in what funds we hoped to be able to amass (e.g., a modest after-tax profit, money for profit sharing). We analyzed historical spending on projects—some of what we did required us to buy or lease equipment—and related that to overall revenue. From this relatively straightforward analysis, we could easily calculate what we needed to sell *at that point in time* to meet all our expenses for that year. That amount became the goal *at that time.*

Each new spending decision then changed what we needed to sell. So, though at any given time we had made our best guesses about the year, we accepted that those guesses would be wrong and would require constant changing. When we contemplated a new expense, regardless of whether it was a new hire or a physical item, we considered what that expense would do to our sales goals. If we weren't able to live with a higher sales goal or with lower profit and less money for profit sharing, then we shouldn't incur the expense.

We went through this sort of analysis quickly because it was not difficult. What made it so simple was a financial practice we'd established in previous organizations and intentionally brought to this new one: complete financial reports every week. Each week, the person—and later, the team—overseeing the company's finances (as we noted, we had someone watching our finances right from the beginning) produces a set of reports that show what has changed financially since the previous week, with notations of all unanticipated expenses, savings, and new income. Basically, it's an income/expense week in review, but one that looks to the rest of the year as well. It also includes an analysis of the always-important cash position of the business. Once you set up the reports, they typically take a small number of hours to produce, and we feel they are well worth the cost.

As we considered spending controls, we realized that we brought a level of detailed knowledge to each decision that we could not reasonably expect everyone in the company to have. More to the point, managing money was a key part of our jobs, and we didn't want to turn everyone in the company into a money manager. No matter how well intentioned or responsible our team members were, they didn't and couldn't reasonably bring to bear on financial decisions the same amount of time and background data as we did.

That line of reasoning, though, led us back to more financial controls than we wanted.

We finally decided to apply to others the same rules we applied to ourselves: discuss before spending, and avoid budgets. We did so, though, with a controlling twist: the discussions had to involve us.

So, if you wanted to spend something, you had to discuss it, typically in email, with us.

discuss before spending, and avoid budgets

At one level, this approach was transparent and open, but at another it felt more controlling to many people than we liked to believe we were. Over time, we encountered the obvious limitations (our time and knowledge) of this approach—more on this in the third part of the book—but we lived with it for a long time, and we are still involved in most significant purchase decisions.

In this area, to some degree we failed, because in a company that tries hard to decentralize control and to trust all of its staffers, we kept a great deal of the financial control with ourselves.

That choice has delivered many benefits, but it has also caused problems. Notably, some people take it as a sign of distrust, of us violating our fundamental statement about believing employees are well-intentioned responsible adults. They argue that they should be able to spend at the speed of business, without question or discussion. Their case is reasonable, and at some level correct. Still, we do believe in having discussions before spending, and that belief is at odds with trusting people.

Thus, the area of financial controls is still ripe for more reinvention.

We did work to streamline financial decisions by creating what amounted to project- or situation-specific projections. When we land a project, we identify all the individual purchases we might have to make for that project, make an estimate of the cost of each (usually, we have that estimate from the process of creating our proposal for the project), and then set aside that money. We don't treat it as a true budget, in that no one can simply spend from it as they want, but rather as a projection for a list of things we expected to need to buy. If a purchase was for an item on that list and at a price similar to our initial projection, the purchase would sail through without discussion. Deviations from the plan, though, would still require discussion.

Similarly, when a staffer is due to get a new laptop, a discussion is necessary, but not with us; a small group of tech folks makes sure the configurations are reasonable.

Today, most purchase decisions happen without our involvement, but we do still participate in the discussions about unplanned, non-project-related expenditures.

We also adopted three unusual practices that help us cultivate a fiscally conservative culture.

One involves bookkeeping. The moment we plan to

spend, we basically mark the amount of money involved as gone. Rather than wait until we get the bill and pay it, a process that can lag the decision by weeks, even months, we treat the decision to spend as the moment to reserve the money. This approach happens to some degree in large organizations at a macro scale via budgets, but we apply it to every spending decision. By doing this, we are never caught off guard by a bill that arrives; we always know our obligations well in advance.

The second is something we call "pre-pay." Because we want to protect our staff and the company as much as possible and be as fiscally conservative as possible, at the end of each year we pay in advance and in full as many large expenses for the next year as we legitimately can. In an era in which banks are paying very little interest on investments, this approach costs us almost nothing—and it often saves us money, because we use the leverage of writing these larger single checks to gain discounts that normal monthly payments would not enjoy. So, we try to pre-pay such things as our rent, our bandwidth contract, our staff health-insurance premiums, and so on. We do this prudently, spending only with vendors we are confident will continue in business and for expenses we know we must incur. In some years, we can pre-pay a great deal; in less successful years, the amount we can pre-pay is more limited.

This approach also can mean that we can begin a year with a great many of our core expenses for the following year already covered. (The biggest single expense line, salaries, of course hits the company at normal paycheck periods.) It also means, though, that what we have to sell in a given year includes the pre-paid expenses for the following year. It took us a number of years before we were in the position to be able to afford this practice, but once we could, we started it. We continue it to this day, though with success that varies from year to year. We monitor the pre-pay obligation just as we do all other fiscal obligations, via the regular weekly reports.

The final unusual practice is one we adopted after we realized that though our industry has no consistent seasonality, we do tend to learn a great deal about how each year is likely to sort out by the end of the first quarter of the year. So, we created a policy of not incurring any discretionary expenses in the first quarter of each year. We'll violate this policy from time to time for purposes such as launching a major business initiative that cannot wait. We also, of course, spend on each project what we need to spend to do the work. Otherwise, however, we buckle down for three months to see how the year is shaking out. If the year looks rough, we stay very tight on discretionary expenses. This approach has helped us protect jobs in tough times.

Each of these practices provides a framework for making financial decisions. Determining guidelines for financial (and other large) decisions can help you move quickly and stay focused.

What we do has worked well for us, but our approaches also have many weaknesses, particularly when it comes to decentralizing control. We have learned that each financial control comes with its own costs—of enforcement, of making some people feel less trusted, of the time of those who are involved in the discussions those controls necessitate.

Whatever controls you choose to institute, create them with thought and with care, and expect to have to change them over time.

Finally, it's vital to make those decisions in calm times, because making good decisions in the heat of stressful moments can be extremely difficult.

each financial control comes with its own costs

CHAPTER 17

deciding before the heat of the moment

In any business, you will inevitably face challenging decisions you must make quickly and with insufficient data. These decisions often are the difference between glowing success, mere survival, and abject failure.

These decisions can happen in both bad situations (how are we going to pay the bills?) and good ones (what should we do with all this money?). Such situations, both good and bad, are also when you may be especially tempted to violate your principles. Creating strong guidelines for your decisions will help you hold true to your beliefs even in those difficult moments.

The guidelines are particularly important for situations that involve substantial amounts of money (the amount will vary depending on the size of the company) and thus provide various degrees of temptation. If, for example, you decide in advance the types of work you will and will not do, then you'll be less likely to be tempted in down times to do something that would go against those principles. Similarly, you should have plans for dealing with layoffs (as we described in a previous chapter), or borrowing money, or evaluating a potentially shady deal in an effort to save the company.

The key in all of these examples is to decide during

more rational times the limits your principles put on what you will do. Put differently, confront in advance the question of what you are willing to do to help your business survive, and what you will do when the business is doing unexpectedly well.

> **decide during more rational times the limits your principles put on what you will do**

We mention both bad and good situations because each provides different temptations. For example, it is a lot harder to be dispassionate about sharing a few million dollars when you are staring at the money; greed may then pose a large temptation. If you've already determined and publicized your profit sharing and spending policies, you simply have to follow them.

We make it a practice of scheduling regular meetings with the two of us to discuss topics such as these, as well as more pressing day-to-day issues. We also try to take at least one trip together each year, typically to TED, and spend time there discussing possible futures and how we would respond to them.

In fact, that was exactly our process and reasoning in deciding the multiplier of sixteen for the compensation difference from the lowest to the highest compensated employees. Deciding that ratio as a theoretical limit was not too difficult. If we had not considered the issue in advance, though, we suspect it would be much harder not to take more money when faced with the possibility.

Letting others know about these advance decisions also can make them easier to follow. After all, deciding to hold to a ratio of sixteen but not telling anyone makes it fairly easy to change the ratio to twenty (or whatever number you want) when you have the opportunity to make additional money. We have the advantage of having each other to hold us accountable, but using broader transparency can also be very helpful.

Making sure everyone understands your guidelines can be particularly important when those guidelines mandate a decision that will be hard on all employees. We once had a client refuse to launch a set of projects unless we did something that would have violated our principles. We were having a rough year, and we very much could have used the money those projects represented. We refused to violate our principles, and we explained why to the whole company in a monthly meeting. Though everyone was acutely aware that the year was rough, the group agreed we should stick to our principles.

The scariest part of making rough decisions in the heat of the moment is that we all have the ability to convince ourselves that we aren't really violating any principles, that what we're doing is okay. Once you do that, it can be very difficult to reclaim your principles, the trust of your customers, the faith of your employees, and, possibly worst, your own self-respect.

A question that touches finances but is also broader is one few businesspeople seem to directly confront: how much baggage do you want your business to accumulate?

CHAPTER 18

travel light

Businesses can easily turn into hoarders. Records that once might have mattered become irrelevant over time but still linger in filing cabinets no one ever opens. Unused office supplies pile up like snow in a blizzard. Furniture and old equipment require storage, and money to pay for the storage, and then people to clean and service that storage.

Similarly, businesses accumulate policies and procedures and rules, sometimes to the point that those things weigh them down, slow them, and hamper their progress.

In other words, businesses tend to travel heavy, carting around an ever-increasing load of baggage. Some of that is unavoidable, because as businesses grow they do need to address issues that didn't matter when they were smaller, but much of what they accumulate is simply unnecessary and adds no value.

Semler wrote about getting rid of a lot of his company's filing cabinets in an effort to remove some of its baggage. We had in our own past enterprises accumulated tons of unnecessary items, things both physical and procedural.

Like many start-ups, PT was going to be a small company in the business of serving very large companies. To do that to the best of its ability, it had to be nimble, fast to respond, and quick to adapt to change—classic virtues that small organizations need to bring to their services to larger ones.

To help it meet those goals, we wanted PT to travel light.

We began with two very mundane notions.

First, we decided that the company would own only one filing cabinet for its records, and that it would do so for at least the first ten years. When we initially made the decision, adhering to it was obviously not a problem. It even became a bit of a joke. As time wore on, though, we accumulated more and more paper, and the cabinet grew more and more full. Somewhere around the seventh year, the folks who managed the HR and financial records said the cabinet was full and asked for a second one.

We said, no, figure it out.

After some consideration, it turned out that we were keeping some records we didn't need to keep, but not many. What they learned, though, was that we could store a great many of our records digitally. That meant scanning a lot of paper and setting up a digital filing system, which cost effectively nothing for the storage and only a modest amount in labor to do all the scanning. We paid the cost. We learned in the process that a great many records we were keeping on paper, notably expense receipts, didn't ever need to be on paper, and so we started encouraging electronic receipt submission. The result was a simpler and faster process with all the benefits of electronic filing, including low cost of storage, ease of backup, and ease of searching. The big savings wasn't in information hoarding—we still have to keep records for tax purposes—but in the time it took many people to file for expenses.

We still have only one filing cabinet for the company's records, and we have no plans to add a second. (We do actually own a second filing cabinet, but only to store client gifts, various company-logoed items, and so on. No one keeps records in it.) When we implement new policies, by reflex we now think about how to store the records they require, how to handle them efficiently, and what we don't need to keep at all. By focusing on a simple target—the accumulation of filing cabinets—we led ourselves to improve our practices.

The second area we tackled was another rather boring one: office supplies. We stocked paper and toner cartridges in the cabinets under printers, because those were expensive, but other than that, our policy with office supplies was simple: if you want it, buy it, and file for reimbursement. We trust you not to buy things you don't need.

That practice lasted for quite some time. We didn't have to buy storage for office supplies, and our costs in those areas stayed extremely low.

One day, though, we happened to notice that a printer cabinet holding a couple of printers contained a drawer with some basic office supplies. When we asked why, the folks on the team that ran HR, finances, and other central admin functions said that people had complained about us not having any supplies, that these folks didn't care a lot about the brands we bought, and that they just wanted to be able to get some basic supplies easily.

So we lost on this one, but not in a bad way. We reminded the team members not to stock many supplies, and to this day, they don't. Our expenses in this area remain extremely low.

In some areas, we've ended up accumulating items, but with good cause. The part of PT that does hands-on product testing frequently needs to compare the newest products with their predecessors. What we tested as new two or three or four years ago becomes the comparison point for tests of today's newer products. So, we keep old hardware. Some, the items the tech folks believe they'll most likely need, stay in the open, while we move others to storage space. Similarly, our video-making teams accumulate props and video and audio equipment.

We continue to push to reduce what we own, but after almost fifteen years we have learned that to do the best possible work for our clients, the company must travel heavier than we had hoped. Still, with this goal in mind, we can travel lighter than we might have otherwise managed.

Another area in which we fight accumulation is in our policies and our work practices. Though these things take no physical space, they still can weigh on the business.

CHAPTER 19

the inevitability of policies

No matter how few policies you want to have, no matter how hard you try to avoid them—and we did try—you will end up with some.

We hate the inevitability of policies, and we resisted it for a long time, but in the end the business must have some policies. The only reason we went as long as we did with as few policies as we had was that we had one uber-policy that addressed many needs: ask the owners. That approach worked when we were small, but it didn't scale. It also placed on the two of us an onus to be consistent, because treating everyone in a company consistently is both the right thing to do and in many realms a legal requirement.

So, with reluctance, we changed our goals from having no or very few policies to having as few policies as we could and to making them as clear, intuitive, and easy to find as possible.

Many policies touch on legal matters, which naturally involve lawyers, who love to write in the difficult to read language of lawyers. We hate that. If you want your company to be as transparent as possible, you have to make its communications as clear as possible. You can ask your lawyers to draw up your policies, but what you'll typically get are huge, complex documents that are anything but clear to anyone who isn't a lawyer. We're very happy with our lawyers, but we have accepted that we often will have to battle with them (and pay them for the privilege).

Consider, for example, our employment agreements. We must have them, and they must contain confidentiality sections, because our clients quite reasonably require us to maintain such commitments for the people who work on their projects. When we asked our lawyers for a draft agreement and stressed how simple we wanted it to be, what they initially sent us ran more than two-dozen pages. We pushed back and worked our way down to a dozen pages. After much discussion and with the understanding that we really did want to treat all employees as well-intentioned responsible adults who want to do good work, we ended up with a couple of straightforward pages and a short rider about the small gym we maintain for employees.

> **create space for the organization to find its best path forward**

One of the ways in which we strive for simplicity is by not creating policies until we need them. We want to create space for the organization to find its best path forward. Balancing this with the goal of making key decisions ahead of time can be tricky, of course, so it's an area we have to monitor carefully.

Travel is a classic area for policies. The travel rules of

many companies are both complex and harsh. We took a different approach: we consider business travel to be a hardship, so want it to be as easy on people as possible. For a long time, very few people traveled for company business. In fact, the traveling group initially consisted of the two of us and a few others who had been with the company for ages. Our policy then was simple: travel is hard, so make it as easy on yourself as you can, but be reasonable. That worked for many years. We all flew coach, because the cost of first-class tickets was unreasonably high. We stayed in nice hotels and often ate at nice restaurants, because those things made the trips nicer without unreasonably inflating costs. A single person booked everyone's travel, because she was good at that task and all involved found it easier to have her do it than to book their own trips. We didn't have any written rules, because we didn't need them.

As we added folks not based in our main office, however, we ended up with many more people traveling. Those people quite reasonably asked for the rules. We had enough people traveling that their definitions of what was reasonable naturally differed. Some of them, for example, greatly preferred booking their own trips. We ended up changing our rules, writing down some basic policies, and allowing people to book their own travel. (We also completely blew the communication process involved in these changes, to the point of unintentionally upsetting some folks. More on some of the lessons we learned from this process in the third part of the book.)

As the company grew, we realized we were making the entire area of policies more difficult than it should be by relying on word of mouth, so we accepted that we would have to document our policies. We went the fairly standard route of creating a secure employee portal and putting on it short, clear write-ups of our policies. Rather than have our lawyers write the text, we assigned the task to the same writers who produce clear copy for our clients. After all, serving our people is one of the reasons we exist, so of course we should use the best writers for the job.

Everyone in the company could now easily find the policies, and we were no longer relying on word of mouth. At the same time, the act of creating this site gave us the opportunity to see all the policies in one place. That led us to wonder whether we really needed them all.

If you want to travel light, and we still constantly strive to do so, you have to regularly check that the policies you have are ones you need, and you have to be willing to alter or even entirely delete ones you no longer require. If a policy is hard to understand, it's either a bad policy or one you've failed to explain well. Similarly, if a policy feels at all counter-intuitive, explain it or change it. If transparency and trusting your fellow employees are to be core corporate principles, as they are for us, you must make sure that each and every policy reflects those principles.

The question becomes, of course, how to do that efficiently. For us, the answer was to aim to commit to a complete review of all policies once a year. We made a group of people relatively new to the policies be the ones who did the review, and we hope to vary the group yearly. We want to bring as many perspectives to bear as possible on these policies, so we gain the benefit of the knowledge of many people in the company. The review team's job is not only to check each policy to make sure it's clear and current, but also to question whether it needs to be there at all. If a policy makes you wonder, "Why do these rules even exist?" maybe the answer is that they shouldn't. Sometimes a key part of traveling light is throwing out what you no longer need.

We have not succeeded in doing this review every year, but that remains our target.

Business practices are like policies in that they also accumulate unavoidably, because all involved in each business area naturally and intelligently want to capture their best practices and train others to follow them. Though it's great to take advantage of these best practices, and capturing them is often essential to productivity, they also pose dangers—and opportunities for reinvention.

Sometimes a key part of traveling light is throwing out what you no longer need.

LIMIT YOUR GREED

CHAPTER 20

reinvent your hits

A set of best practices for solving a particular problem is basically a recipe. A recipc is a good thing, because it helps you achieve the same, or at least a very similar, result repeatedly and with minimal cost. It can also, however, become a substitute for thinking about fresh approaches to a problem. To do great work, you have to constantly reap the benefits of what you have learned from hard experience. At the same time, if you don't try new techniques and approaches, you can end up paying the costs of missing the improvements they might deliver.

The best way to achieve that balance is to regularly review these practices.

Keeping with the goal of traveling light, each review should begin with the same key question: Why are we doing this? The answer, "Because we've always done it," is not acceptable. If you're expending energy or money or time, it should be because you gain something in return for that investment. It doesn't matter if the cost is low or if the least expensive person in the company is doing the work; if a practice doesn't deliver value, stop it. If by established practices you circulate a type of document to people on three different teams and representatives of one of those teams never respond, ask if they still want to see those documents. If you regularly attend meetings but find they're running fine without you, bow out.

Never do anything just because you used to do it.

Never do anything just because you used to do it.

If you're wondering if a practice delivers value, or even if you're not sure, ask the people for whom you're implementing the practice. If you've always delivered something to your clients in four different formats, ask them if they want all those formats. If you're offering a service to your employees but don't notice anyone taking advantage of it, ask them if they still want it.

When in doubt, ask. Listening closely to those you serve is the best way to learn what you should and should not be doing.

If a business practice does deliver value, then periodically review your best practices to make sure they are current and as good as you can reasonably make them. With practices that involve technology products, this is particularly important, because those products are constantly evolving—and sometimes better ones replace them entirely. Of course, change comes with its own costs—the expense of making the change, the time to do any necessary retraining, and so on—so be sure to factor those costs into your analysis.

Finally, even if a practice is clearly of value, even if all the people for whom you are doing it like it, consider whether you could do it better.

This same thinking applies to your products, whether those products are items or services. Your sales will, of course, alert you to your failures, so you'll know you need to cancel and/or replace the things that failed. What your sales often won't tell you early enough is when your hits are losing their luster.

Always look for ways to reinvent your hits.

As soon as an item or service becomes a huge hit, you should be thinking about what will come after it. Buyers are fickle, because everyone wants the next new great thing. Your competitors will certainly be analyzing your hits and doing their best to create better offerings; you should do the same. Talk to your customers to learn what they most like and what they most dislike about your hits, as well as what they wish you would do. Use what you learn to create even more great products and services.

One of the truths of our business is that whatever services we are providing most today, whatever is hottest now, is probably going to be a minority offering in eighteen months to two years. When we have a sure-fire winner, we always start trying to figure out how to replace it with something even better. Do this, and your customers will both get better products and come to expect you to listen to their needs and innovate accordingly.

Everyone wins.

To this point, we've talked about different ways to approach the creation and operation of businesses, and we've shared some of what has worked well in the business and social experiment that is PT. We haven't yet talked much about some of the challenges—and, we hope, opportunities—we have faced and are facing as we've grown.

Let's start with a tricky one: evolving our organization—or lack thereof—as the business grows.

PART THREE

Challenges and opportunities

LIMIT YOUR GREED

CHAPTER 21

working to maintain our unusual culture

Though we still don't have an org chart, we definitely have more of an organizational structure than the lack of an org chart might imply. Our guess is that if you ask anyone in the company who their boss is, they'll have a ready answer. Further, they could all draw some sort of org chart. We suspect not all of the charts would show the exact same structure, yet none of them would be entirely wrong, because each would represent the one that is working for the person who drew it. The very fluidity and variability of that structure is a good thing, one of the features of not worrying about creating titles and org charts in the first place.

Still, despite beginning with the goal of avoiding a classic organization, we have evolved a structure.

The fact that people could point to other employees they see as their bosses suggests that leaders did indeed emerge, as we had hoped and expected. We certainly also helped cultivate and assist those who stepped up as leaders, but those people did the hard work of growing and taking on more and more responsibilities. That's all to the good.

As of this writing, the company comprises about ninety people. Six of those people (two of whom are us) participate in the monthly staff reviews we will explain in the next chapter, so you could argue that we've reached a roughly 14:1 ratio of staff to leaders. That's not exactly correct, though, because the organization is much more dynamic than that. We have many more leaders in different teams all around the company; it's simply that only those six people currently participate in the monthly staff reviews and deal with salaries in their areas.

We're still reaping the benefits of dynamic teams that reassemble as necessary, but as we've grown and added different types of work to our practice, we've also had to develop different operating groups within the company. The technical, studio, and support teams in PT each have an overall lead and have evolved different ways of approaching many aspects of their work, ways suitable to their jobs. In general, that's good, but it has brought us the challenge of building a culture that works for very different types of people who regularly need to work in different ways. That was always going to happen, but now working to maintain our unusual culture is something we have to do almost every day. We also have other teams, such as our growing development group, that currently don't fit within any of the existing major teams.

Making our organizational challenge greater is the fact that the groups frequently participate in very different types of projects. For example, the people in our studio team work on everything from projects involving product testing to those centered on e-learning course development.

Avoiding us versus them intra-company conflicts is a

related, key challenge. As we said earlier, we built PT around the notion that we're all in it together, that we all win or lose together. That attitude is easy to sustain for everyone when everyone is doing basically the same type of work. When you have different types of teams doing different types of work, and some teams contributing much more income than others, you start having the potential for resentment and conflict. (You can't avoid this issue, alas, because at a minimum you will need some support people, and those people typically do not work on billable projects.) To avoid that conflict, everyone in the company should appreciate the value that all their co-workers, not just the ones in their particular areas, bring to the business. Communicating that value across the organization is a constant challenge.

None of these challenges apply to just the leaders, either; all of them are challenges every individual in the company faces. In any corporate culture, but particularly in an unusual one, each person in the company carries some of the weight of sustaining that culture.

each person in the company carries some of the weight of sustaining that culture.

Similarly, every person in a company is a cultural ambassador to each new person you hire. Those new people will have a hard enough time figuring out the culture even if all the messages they receive are consistent. If the people they work with give very different takes on key attributes of your culture, the newer folks will understandably find it very hard to figure out what your business is about and how to work in it.

Communication is once again critical and an area in which we find ourselves having to constantly improve.

A particular challenge of good communication is identifying the right mechanisms for providing feedback, both positive and negative, to employees.

CHAPTER 22

providing frequent feedback

The lighter the organization's structure, the easier it is to ignore the importance of giving employees sufficient feedback. When you have an org chart that identifies managers, those people probably review the people they manage. When you create an organization as fluid as ours, if you're not careful you may find no one has the explicit task of doing reviews. Reviews are vital, however, if you want to help your employees grow and reach their full potentials.

In most organizations, the mechanism for this feedback is a combination of an annual review, at which people typically receive raises in years in which the business is giving raises, and less structured feedback that is supposed to happen in the course of day-to-day work. In our experience, in most organizations what really happens is that employees receive feedback only at those annual reviews or when they've clearly messed up in the eyes of the person doing their reviews.

When we were small, feedback was simple, because we were all working closely together and so would talk about pretty much everything. As we grew, that informal system stopped working well, and we had to develop a more structured one. It also became increasingly obvious how difficult it was for new hires to transition from a typical business environment to our more unusual one, so we had to pay special attention to those people.

Over time, we evolved a system that seemed to work pretty well. Everyone on staff received an annual review, of course. That review always included the two of us, to make sure each employee always got time with the owners, as well as the lead of the area in which they worked. Each employee also received a quarterly review that included the lead for their area and one of the two of us. New staff members received a review every month until we and they felt they were comfortable in our system and they could move to quarterly feedback. In addition, each month we asked the entire staff for any input they had on their co-workers. The main point of that request was for nominations for performance bonuses, but we invited feedback of all sorts. We asked that people send their feedback to an email list whose members were the company's leaders. All feedback stayed confidential to that group.

This approach, though it worked well for some time and provided fairly frequent feedback to all, had the same obvious problem as many of our initial mechanisms: we two became bottlenecks. The sheer number of employees and our other responsibilities made it increasingly difficult for us to attend all the reviews. We also were not in many cases the people with the most knowledge about the performance of the people in many reviews.

The system that had once worked felt like it was breaking.

In the spirit of serving our employees well and listening to them, we conducted a survey of the whole company on the topic of reviews. (More on surveys in the next chapter.) After reading and thinking about all their input, we created and announced a new review system. This one has the people with the most knowledge of a person's performance provide the key input to that person's review, but it also incorporates other goals people expressed, such as the chance to talk occasionally with the two of us. The new system includes thrice-yearly reviews and a bunch of other changes. So far, it appears to be working well, but we will soon do another survey and ask people how they feel about it and what we could do better.

Ask, listen, and strive to serve better—basic PT principles.

As you might expect by now, we have avoided any sort of formal ratings or forms for evaluating people. While we can see some value in them, especially as we have increased the size of the group of people conducting the reviews, on balance we've found such mechanisms tend to not be very helpful. In most organizations, they seem to become less about growing people and more about putting people into boxes for either promotion or firing.

We have also learned that our periodic reviews may not be frequent or well-timed enough when an employee is having trouble in their job. This is particularly true in a constantly shifting organization where you can have difficulty telling if a problem is the person in question or just the perception of someone who worked with that person recently.

We have found some success in such situations by linking people with different leaders, providing them new mentors, or changing the kind of work they're doing, but we still need to improve in this area.

Sometimes, despite all of our best efforts, we have had to fire people. As much as we hate it, sometimes it's necessary. Our only real advice here is what we mentioned earlier: make sure you have given the person in question more than enough chances to fix their performance issues. We are not talking here, of course, about someone stealing from the company or physically assaulting a colleague, situations in which firing is relatively simple and clearly the right choice. Instead, we are discussing how to handle people who may be trying but who just can't get things right. In such cases, you are better off wasting some money and effort on a person than getting rid of that person too soon. By putting in this extra effort and giving troubled employees extra time, we've enjoyed multiple success stories in which people turned into valued employees—in some cases even though they were partway through the firing process.

When we do have to fire someone, even someone we know is not doing good work, it feels bad. It feels like failure.

It should.

Firing, even when it's necessary, should always feel bad. When it stops

> **Firing, even when it's necessary, should always feel bad.**

feeling bad, or just stops causing any feelings, you have a strong indication that something is wrong either in the organization or with you.

As we mentioned and as you'd expect from a company that values all employees and wants all of them involved in shaping it, as part of the reviews process we gave everyone in the company a chance to express their thoughts on how reviews should work. In fact, we regularly sought everyone's input on a lot of different company topics.

Trying to do that raised another challenge: how do you make sure everyone feels safe about speaking up?

LIMIT YOUR GREED

CHAPTER 23

a way for people to communicate their thoughts

We thought we had created a culture of open communication, and to a large degree we had. With a monthly all-hands company meeting and monthly email messages inviting everyone to give feedback on their co-workers, we thought we were clear about wanting to hear what people thought. We also considered ourselves to be open to talking about pretty much anything with anyone and everyone on the staff. From our perspective, all of those viewpoints were correct.

It's easy to forget, however, that people see the world very differently. It's also easy to think your environment is a safe one for open communication when you hold the highest level of power in an organization.

The perspectives of other people, particularly but not only newer employees, can be quite different. People may simply be bashful about speaking up in a group. They might have serious concerns and valuable input but for whatever reason worry that sharing their thoughts might upset someone they perceive to be more powerful than they are.

As we grew and considered these issues more fully, we realized that if we truly wanted to foster open communication, we had to find a way for people to share their thoughts and always feel safe doing so. We considered all sorts of announcements and mechanisms, and we spoke openly and often about inviting and wanting more feedback, but ultimately, we came to understand that for some people the only way to feel safe was to be able to give their feedback anonymously.

Fortunately, anonymity is a relatively easy issue to tackle with modern technology.

After some research, we settled on a survey tool that would meet our requirements of letting each employee opine only once—no stuffing the ballot box for any of us—and do so anonymously. We announced early in 2014 that we would start doing anonymous monthly surveys of all staff on a variety of topics—including periodically asking what else we should be doing surveys on.

The surveys are short and always optional. Most months, we do one survey, and the next month we report its results—all of its results, regardless of what they say about the company. A writer makes a pass over the write-in portion of the results to remove any content that might be offensive or hurtful to others in the company. Such content is rare but does occasionally appear, most commonly as curse words. Otherwise, we present the results to the whole company as they are.

Participation has ranged from just a few members of the staff to over two thirds of it, though most of the time it is under half. We've learned a great deal from some of the surveys and, predictably, less from others. We've also made a lot of changes based on what people said in those surveys.

One of the obvious lessons the surveys have brought home—not just to us, but also to the whole company—is that you can't make everyone happy with everything. Everyone knows this truism, but it's easy to forget when you're passionate about something. People are generally more accepting of not getting their way when they're out-voted by a majority and can see proof of that fact. When you share more information, you make clear not only why you did what you did, but also at least some of the complexities of the situation.

> **you can't make everyone happy with everything**

Another aspect of open communication that we hadn't fully embraced is that sometimes the discussion is more important than the decision. Put differently, people sometimes simply want to be heard.

As we mentioned in the previous section of the book, we learned that several folks weren't happy with some aspects of our travel policy. We helped foster what we intended to be a safe space for those people to have a discussion—a space that did not include us—so they could say whatever they wanted without worrying that we might not like it. When they were done, they sent us their recommendations. From our perspective, we basically said, "Yes" to those recommendations, and we thought the discussion was over. We believed we'd done as they wanted, and we expected everyone to be happy.

Except they weren't. They very much weren't.

Once we learned of their unhappiness, we reviewed the process with them. As it turns out, we had done several things wrong. First, in giving our own thoughts on the policy to them, something we did informally as we were letting them know the results of their recommendations, we created a narrative that felt confrontational, even punitive, to them. We also didn't really understand their requests, so what we said "Yes" to was not actually what they wanted. Perhaps most importantly, we never held the follow-up discussion they quite reasonably expected would happen. By saying, "Yes," we thought we were giving them what they wanted. Instead, we were failing them by not having a conversation and not working toward an answer together.

In a company that prizes discussions about important topics, we had failed to notice the need for a discussion.

We eventually had that conversation. It was a good and enlightening one for all of us. We all learned ways in which we hadn't communicated well, and we changed and improved our travel policies.

Some people with whom we've discussed our focus on improving communication have countered that we're babying people and that those people should just grow up and live in the real world, where bosses make decisions and employees have to live with them (or words to those effects). That's certainly the perspective of many companies, but we disagree with it. Yes, ultimately, we all have to live with the decisions a company makes, but that doesn't mean you can't all talk first. If you want everyone to feel invested in the company, and if you truly value and want to understand everyone's thoughts and perspectives, you may need to hold more conversations. Those conversations don't have to be long, and you certainly can't afford for them to unreasonably slow the pace of business, but they're important.

Fostering open communication is difficult, but the results are worth the effort.

Another tricky area, and one in which we continue to have to improve, is balancing the desire for a lean operation, one with tight financial controls, with the goal of trusting all the employees, the people we continue to believe are well-intentioned responsible adults who want to do good work.

If you truly value and want to understand everyone's thoughts and perspectives, you may need to hold more conversations.

LIMIT YOUR GREED

CHAPTER 24

having discussions before spending

Forcing a discussion around spending requests was, from our perspective and as we discussed earlier, a sound practice and one that felt to us both transparent and open. As we also mentioned, this approach came across to many others rather differently: as controlling and, worse, as untrusting. We had good reasons for not simply allowing anyone to spend whatever they wanted, and we outlined those earlier, but as we grew, our solution proved less and less workable.

It obviously doesn't scale. If the owners have to be involved in every purchase decision, then simple math shows that at some point in a company's growth that becomes all they do—and then it becomes more than they can do. Decentralizing control becomes an imperative.

So we did. We started the practice of reserves (money put aside for anticipated spending) for projects. We created groups that reviewed certain types of common purchases, such as new laptops for employees. The support team took on the task of asking for explanations for spending requests and suggesting cheaper sources for fulfilling the requests. And so on.

Those changes greatly reduced the load on us, but we

are still too involved in purchasing. We need to further lessen our involvement.

The changes also still left some people feeling untrusted—and, worse, some of those people were our leaders. From their perspective, if we trusted them to lead lots of projects and essentially run major chunks of the company, why didn't we trust them to spend money?

From our perspective, the issue wasn't about trust, it was about having conversations, making sure we brought all the key perspectives to each spending discussion, and generally avoiding spending whenever reasonably possible. As we try to remind people regularly, one of the easiest ways to boost profit sharing and profit in general is to keep expenses low.

> one of the easiest ways to boost profit sharing and profit in general is to keep expenses low

The changes also made the support team in some ways an adversary of the other teams. That's a common enough situation in most companies, but it's not how we want things to be. Constantly making sure we're all pulling for the same goals and recognizing that we're all in it together remain key focuses.

Finally, forcing discussions can have the unfortunate side effect of slowing the pace of work, and that's something no small company should take lightly. We all recognize the need for lightweight, high-speed solutions.

As one possible answer, multiple leaders proposed relatively low (say, $500 or $1,000) spending limits, so that any purchase requests from those people that fell at or below those limits would flow through the system without question.

We weren't fully comfortable with that approach for three reasons. It amounts to creating mini-budgets (earlier, we gave our reasons for disliking budgets). We resist whenever we reasonably can actions that create classes of employees, which this would do on the spending front. Most of all, we continue to believe in having discussions before spending.

We have yet to come up with a great solution in this area. We know we must further decentralize control, and we definitely trust our people and want them to feel trusted. We also want those involved in spending to discuss the reasons and to be able to bring strong financial knowledge into those discussions. Though we may end up with a more conventional financial approach, we want to do better than that if we possibly can. In this area, that's a particularly tough goal.

No one said reinventing business would be easy.

Meanwhile, even as we wrestled with issues involving our current staff, we had to face a challenge in finding new people.

LIMIT YOUR GREED

CHAPTER 25

work to achieve meaningful diversity

As part of our discussion of our fundamental attitudes about employees, we touched briefly on our practice of frequently trying to hire people we knew and the benefits of doing so. We also mentioned a serious drawback of this approach: as a company, we were not as diverse as we wanted to be.

The virtues of employee diversity are many and are the topic of a wide range of articles, discussions, and research activities today. We're not going to attempt to summarize or debate them here. For this book's purposes, suffice to say that we have come to believe that actively embracing diversity is important, very important, both for our society as a whole and for our own business.

If you're starting or running a small business, it's easy to think of diversity as an issue only for larger enterprises, but we believe that's a mistake. Diversity is important in companies of all sizes, especially those looking to think differently and reinvent the way they do business.

We approached the topic of improving diversity slowly, largely by observing our business' characteristics as it grew. Initially, most of the people we hired were of similar ages, people at least a decade and frequently further into their careers. We responded by making an effort to attract and hire people of a broader range of ages, with an emphasis on younger people. As of this writing, almost sixty percent of the staff is under forty, and a little over a quarter is under thirty. We have employees in every age decade from their twenties to their sixties.

We were also aware of and quite concerned about the problem of the diminishing participation of women and minorities in STEM (Science, Technology, Engineering, and Math) fields. As a company with a large technical team, we very much wanted to buck that trend. On the surface, we've done okay in one area, because almost 35% of our staff is female. Unfortunately, relatively few members of our technical testing staff are female, but the majority of our development team is female. So, we made progress, but we have a great deal more work to do here.

We've done worse with representation of people of color, though we are better than we once were. Today, people of color are a bit over 10% of the company. We clearly need to improve a great deal in this area.

Discrimination is not only illegal; it's stupid.

We have, of course, always tried to hire the best candidates for the job, with no discrimination of any sort. Discrimination is not only illegal; it's stupid. Why wouldn't any business want the best possible people for the job? What we weren't doing was making enough of an effort to solicit a broader variety of people. Our established hiring practices helped us fill job openings quickly, and we were finding great people, but we weren't actively working to increase our diversity. As Mellody Hobson exhorted in her TED 2014 talk,[1] it's not enough to be color blind; you also need to be color brave. "We have to be willing," she said, "as teachers and parents and entrepreneurs and scientists, we have to be willing to have proactive conversations about race with honesty and understanding and courage, not because it's the right thing to do, but because it's the smart thing to do, because our businesses and our products and our science, our research, all of that will be better with greater diversity." We wanted to accept that challenge and knew we would have to work hard and change our policies if we were to achieve meaningful diversity.

After TED, we discussed this topic in a company meeting and asked for volunteers to form a committee to improve our diversity. We didn't approve the committee's membership. To the best of our knowledge, no one did. Instead, those who cared enough to give it their time—and this was definitely bonus work; each person's other workload stayed the same—joined the committee. It produced a set of recommendations for future hiring. We followed those recommendations in some hiring but not in all; sometimes we by-passed them in the interest of speed. We are

[1] http://www.ted.com/talks/mellody_hobson_color_blind_or_color_brave

now in the process of refining them and committing to following the new standards.

Attacking this challenge, like dealing with most challenges, is not free. It costs. For example, we now post job openings in a far broader variety of places and leave them open for a longer time than in the past. Our support staff thus has to spend more time sorting through and responding to applications, and sometimes we have to pay more to keep up our job postings. We believe, though, that the benefits of becoming more diverse will outweigh the costs. After all, we work in an increasingly diverse world serving an increasingly diverse set of clients, so both our employees and our clients will win as we increase our own diversity.

Part of the challenge in finding the best possible new employees, even for a business dedicated to being a great place to work, is making sure people know about the business. Not every company can be a household name and have the instant attraction to a broad base of candidates of, for example, Google or Apple. Smaller companies have to consider seriously how they are willing to market themselves to potential candidates.

CHAPTER 26

publicity is a bad motivation

For most of PT's existence, we have avoided publicity about the company. Sure, we were doing things we considered good that we liked telling folks about, but we didn't want to appear to be bragging or give the impression that we did these things simply for the publicity they would bring. We had gone to plenty of effort to be a company with great benefits, but we had never cared about being recognized as such. The right reason to do good things, we regularly reminded ourselves and the entire company, is because they are right, not because you are seeking a reward for doing them.

We found, however, that when we told people about what PT was doing, many of them got excited. One example was that upon telling a woman in a non-work context about our sabbatical program, she declared that she wanted to work at a place like that. We had an opening, and now she's on the PT team. Without telling her about the company, she would never have found us.

It became obvious that talking about our company was a good recruiting tool. We, like other companies, are frequently trying to find great people, and the more tools that can help us do that, the better. So, we found ourselves deciding with some reluctance to have PT participate in a contest a local business publication held to identify the best places to work in the area. PT has ranked in the top fifteen best places to work for all four years we've participated. While doing well in rankings like these is gratifying, our main goal was to help us recruit the best people as we continued to grow.

We also felt that by publicizing what our company and its people do, we might be able to positively affect other companies. Sharing our sabbatical program in conversations, for example, has made a lot of people talk seriously about how their businesses might do similar things.

> **We also felt that by publicizing what our company and its people do, we might be able to positively affect other companies.**

One day, after discussing our sabbatical program and how to make it even better, we made the easy (in retrospect) observation that we were now in the video-production business, so we should make a short video about each employee's sabbatical experiences. As we noted earlier in the book, this practice is now our standard. We host those videos on our site and on our YouTube channel (check them out by searching there for "PT sabbaticals").

To further help each of the charities for which our employees worked, we give each such charity the full rights to use the video as it chooses, including for fundraising. We debut the videos for the entire PT staff, so everyone in the company can see what the labor they expended to cover for someone on sabbatical helped that person do for the world. Our hope is that the videos will help the charities and also spread the word to other companies about the benefits of a sabbatical program that encourages people to help make the world a better place.

We now also participate in the usual social media outlets to let the world know about what we and our people are doing. We've come to understand that hiding what we do is not necessarily the best choice for both us and others.

We must again stress that the reason to create programs such as our sabbaticals or our charity donation program is because you believe they are the right things to do. Doing them to get publicity is a bad choice.

What finally led us to tell people about PT's programs, to participate in the contest we mentioned, and to do many other things is that we came to believe we could make a greater difference in the world by doing so.

That same motivation led us to write this book.

We've saved the two biggest challenges for last, in part because we are only beginning to address them directly, and in part because we have the fewest answers for them right now.

Let's start with one that affects everyone in every business: work/life balance.

LIMIT YOUR GREED

CHAPTER 27

work/life balance is still a challenge

The tech industry is justifiably famous—and infamous—for being demanding. Tales of employees working long days for months of crunch times are legion. Tech isn't the only part of the U.S. economy, though, where workers are putting in a lot of hours. An August 2014 Gallup poll pegged the average number of work hours per week for salaried U.S. employees at 47.[2] Work/life balance is a challenge all over the U.S.

Our company is no exception. Though the reported average number of hours that PT employees work is below that figure, it's still over 40, and during crunches quite a few people will average a great many hours more than that per week. We tend to work hard, and we value hard work.

None of this is surprising. We expect that to be the case for a small business, particularly a small tech business. As we've indicated, we compensate people well, we have performance bonuses for those who go above and beyond, and we're all keenly aware that money we save by not having to hire more people can become available for profit sharing. Our sabbaticals definitely help, but they come only every seven years.

---

2 Lydia Saad, "The "40-Hour" Workweek Is Actually Longer — by Seven Hours," accessed October 29, 2017, http://www.gallup.com/poll/175286/hour-workweek-actually-longer-seven-hours.aspx

Extreme work hours—and we are both guilty of regularly having them—wear on people (including us), both physically and mentally. At the same time, our ability to accomplish a great deal in a short time—an ability that comes in part from people putting in those extra hours—is something our clients count on, part of the service that a small company needs to be able to provide its large clients. Being nimble and resourceful and very hard working is part of the game.

We have no easy answers to offer here.

We do have some clear concerns and observations.

Though as we noted earlier, our company by all modern definitions has an unlimited vacation policy, we worry that many people don't take enough time off. We don't actually know how much time off each person takes, because we truly don't track it; that comes with the unlimited vacation territory. We do, however, know of at least some people who are not taking sufficient time off, at least in our eyes.

We also know that the blurring of the lines between work time and personal time has led some people to feel they can never

> the blurring of the lines between work time and personal time has led some people to feel they can never be away and must always be available for work.

be away and must always be available for work. That feeling is draining and not a good thing for anyone.

Because we do have to track all project-related hours, we have good data on how much each person is working each month. As you would expect, the extra work hours aren't evenly distributed across the entire staff. Those people who step up most—the leaders, the gurus, the driven ones— tend to log the most work time, though most people put in extra work when necessary. The willingness to go the extra mile in many ways is a key trait of great players on teams of all sorts, but it also makes those people more likely to suffer fatigue and burnout.

We have made some efforts to address this issue by doing things like the "soft close" during the last two weeks of the year, and in 2016 we experimented with hard closes over some key holidays. Our hope is that with most folks off, even the more driven folks will take time off. We feel, however, that we still need to do more.

What we know for sure is that improving in this area will cost us all, though we're not yet sure in exactly which ways. It seems likely, for example, that if we want to limit our hours further, we may all need to limit our greed further and accept smaller profit-sharing payments.

We also know that we won't solve this problem on our own. We have surveyed the entire company, and the responses were varied, interesting, and demanded close study. We will continue to discuss the topic with everyone, probably multiple times, so that if and when we do make changes, they will reflect an understanding of what we as a group want to do.

The final challenge is also one that affects everyone in the company, albeit in many cases indirectly, but it directly involves two people: us.

CHAPTER 28

in the absence of an exit plan, how do you exit?

We mentioned early in the book that we intentionally created PT without an exit plan for ourselves. We did not want to focus on selling the company or taking it public or in any way maximizing shareholder return. We created a business that existed to do great work for its clients and to be a great place to work for its employees. We decided to figure out the rest later

After fifteen years of doing this and growing older, we have finally had to confront an obvious question: in the absence of an exit plan, how do you exit?

If you own a business, you have to consider this question eventually, because whether we want to or not, we all exit—not just the business, but life itself—eventually.

This question immediately raises a host of other important questions, including the following:

Do you want the company to continue without you?

Who will own the company when you leave? When you die?

Who will run the company when you're not doing so?

How do you transition the company's operations to those people?

How will you ensure the company stays true to its

culture when you're gone? Should that even be a goal? Is that one of your goals?

Selfishly, how do you get back some value from this company you created and own?

We started considering this topic by contemplating the first and last questions in the above list.

> **How do you get back some value from this company you created and own?**

An easy way to answer both is to sell the company. Then, you get a return on your investment, one you could share with employees if you chose to do so—and we most certainly would. Whether the company would continue under its new owners really would not be something you could control.

As we've noted in this book—as, in fact, this book's very existence demonstrates—PT is more to us than just a company. It's a social experiment, a living lab in which we've tried to reinvent and improve business. It is in some small way a vehicle for doing good in the world. It is a family. We care deeply about it.

So, we quickly decided that we wanted the company to continue without us. We equally quickly decided that we were not out to sell the company.

At this point, we feel obliged to say that given the right offer, we would sell. Such an offer, however, would have to be for a sufficiently large sum that we could give each employee enough to ensure they would have the ability to leave if the new owners did not treat them well. This approach should motivate any purchaser to continue the company's unusual culture and to treat its people well. We consider such an outcome as possible, but not likely.

How, then, were we to get value from the company we had created and still owned? We've said we're capitalists and like money, but without selling the company, getting money from it is difficult.

As you might know, many businesses specialize in helping owners deal with this problem. The most common techniques amount to selling the company to its employees, either via individual purchases of stock or by saddling the company with debt. We doubted whether our staff could pay a reasonable value for the company, and saddling it with debt goes against our fiscally conservative spirits.

After much consideration, we are currently attempting to do something rather different: to accept that in all likelihood we will never get back from the company anywhere near what it is worth. We started with the assumption that limiting our greed could lead to good results, and we believe it has. We're going to continue limiting our greed. We're working to phase ourselves out slowly, but we're planning to stay on as employees with salaries and benefits. So, we—and, eventually, our heirs—will make some money each year from the company, but we most likely won't make all that the company is worth. We'll limit our greed so that PT can continue to do great work for its clients and be a great place to work for its staff.

If this notion proves to be workable, then we will continue to follow it. If it does not, then we'll again evaluate our options and try to find the best path forward for both us and everyone else at PT.

As for the other questions, we'll work them out as we do everything else: by involving the entire company, making sure the culture remains what we and they want it to be, and doing our best to ensure that whatever we do makes PT continue to be a great place to work for them.

After all, if they win, we win. We're all in it together.

PART FOUR

Afterwords

LIMIT YOUR GREED

BILL'S AFTERWORD

"Leaf by Niggle"

As we've touched on a number of times in this book, when we tell people about PT, they often have the obvious "why" questions. For example, why did you create a business this way? And why did you feel compelled to write about it?

My main impetus for creating this business this way is my belief in Christian Biblical principles. I believe they should, and indeed must, influence all areas of my life, including how I conduct myself in the workplace and what kind of workplace I might try to create

At the simplest level, we were all created to work. In Genesis, God's creation efforts are described as work, and the Bible says that He rested from His work when it was completed. Further, His created beings were commanded to work to maintain His creation. From the very beginning, we were meant to work.

Tim Keller, in his excellent book *Every Good Endeavor*, does a masterful job of describing the intrinsic value of work based on Biblical principles. He states, "Work is as much a basic human need as food, beauty, rest, friendship, prayer, and sexuality. Without meaningful work we sense significant inner loss and emptiness. People who are cut off from work because of physical or other reasons quickly discover how much they need work to thrive emotionally, physically, and spiritually."

The problem is that many jobs and companies rob work of its value. Instead of bringing worth and sustenance to an individual, the job and its work bring sorrow and toil.

My desire is that our company might help people find the fulfilling, meaningful work that they were created to do. Though most of the ideas we implemented at PT and described in this book came from both of us, they incorporate some very Biblical concepts. As an example, the word sabbatical has its roots in the Old Testament concept of the Sabbath, or rest. This concept of mandated rest referred not only to the Sabbath, or seventh day of the week (a day of rest), but also to the Sabbath, or seventh, year, when even the fields were allowed to rest. We did not choose our sabbatical program based strictly upon those principles, but they certainly resonated with me.

Similarly, I view principles like servant leadership, egalitarianism, caring for the needs of other people, and most of the others we discuss in this book as both Biblically sound and good business.

Even if PT has been a great experiment that has allowed me to try to practice what I believe, why did I feel compelled to tell others about it and the rationale behind it?

In truth, I think we've put off writing the book so long that we are running out of time. I feel a bit like Niggle, the central character in J.R.R. Tolkien's allegorical story, "Leaf by Niggle." Niggle spent years trying to finish a painting of a tree that he felt compelled to paint. Lots of things got in the way, both big things and small things, both good things and bad things. Ultimately, Niggle is too late and does not get to finish his painting of a tree, just some of the leaves. Nonetheless, it turned out that what he did manage to paint had a great impact on others.

My hope is that by writing this book, I can be a bit like Niggle and influence the world in a positive way. Even if I know I could have and should have done more, maybe if folks see that a company like Principled Technologies is possible, they will change their business principles. If so, then like Niggle, I may be able to see some of my dreams realized by others.

Amen.

LIMIT YOUR GREED

MARK'S AFTERWORD

Every little bit helps

When I was a teenager, I wanted to change the world. I had grand dreams of doing great things, but those dreams were fuzzy creations lacking solidity and focus. As I marched through junior high and high school and college and grad school, the dreams remained with me but never dominated my time, most of which went to doing whatever task was in front of me. I got a job and then another, and then I started my first company. Along the way, I wrote stories and then novels—I still write novels—and hoped that they might both entertain and touch people.

In the years between then and now, I realized that all of us change the world, even if only our little parts of it, with how we behave, what we do, and what we say. We don't always realize we're doing it, but we're always affecting other people, altering a tiny corner of our collective reality with our presence.

When we started PT, I wanted more than just a way to make money. Finding a job would have been easy. Even starting a company would have been simple enough; as I said, I'd done it before. I wanted more. I wanted to go back to those young dreams and to try to change the world—even if only my little corner of it. Bill was similarly inspired. As much as I love writing and have written on a broad variety of topics, I didn't just want to write about how businesses could be better; I wanted to prove it was possible to create new and better types of companies. Bill and I agreed that from its name to its every action, we wanted to build a company that would demonstrate by its very existence that you *can* build a good business without following the traditional paths, that you can do well and not be a slave to the bottom line.

As much as it would be nice to claim we had it all figured out from the start, we didn't. We learned as we went. We started with the existence statement we discussed early in this book, and we figured out the rest as we went along.

After nearly fifteen years in operation, we have solid proof that it's possible to build a business that is both profitable and focused foremost and relentlessly on caring for its clients and its employees. We know for certain that you can build such businesses, because we've built one.

Over the years of PT's existence, we've talked about it with a great many people. The vast majority of them have said how good it sounded—and how it probably wouldn't work for their business, or their market.

I disagree.

With this book, I want to show *a* path—not *the* path, just one of many possible paths—to creating a business that truly places people first. I want to share what we've learned so that you might build your own new, better businesses.

I want to change more of the world than PT can touch. I want to show that making money does not have to come at the expense of treating people well, that doing great work for clients is in no way in opposition to being a great place to work for employees, and that all of this is possible now, in the real world, in the market we all face, with the realities we all battle.

Yes, you have to be willing to accept less money than you might otherwise make—to limit your greed—but if you are, if you will share more and live with less, then you can make the world—or at least your little part of it—a better place for you and for others. If you make that choice, you will still have the chance to earn good money, but more importantly, your heart will be richer for what you've done.

I hope you do.

ABOUT THE AUTHORS

Mark L. Van Name and Bill Catchings are writers, technologists, and business owners. Over the course of over thirty years of working together, they have published more than a thousand articles on technology and founded and led multiple companies. Principled Technologies, their current primary business, has been following the principles of this book for its entire fifteen-year existence. Van Name and Catchings live and work in the Research Triangle Park area of North Carolina.

We set this book in the Karmina face, which the
TypeTogether foundry created. Karmina is a highly legible
and economic typeface, perfect for extended reading.

Printed and bound by
Sheridan,
Chelsea, Michigan

Designed by
Principled Technologies, Inc.,
Durham, North Carolina